Growth, Equity, and Self-Reliance

About the Book and Editors

This book explores what is, for many African countries, a new and controversial policy of relying on private actors rather than on government organizations to foster economic growth and development. The contributors explore key issues such as the impact of private enterprise on the development process, small- and medium-sized businesses as a vehicle for growth, and strategies for the expansion of markets and trade. The contributors analyze the historical, social, cultural, and economic obstacles to the development of private enterprise in Africa; the roles of government, women, and business organizations; access to capital and the function of financial institutions; private initiative and agriculture; the use of skilled and semi-skilled labor; and technology transfer. Arguing that private sector forces are crucial to African socio-economic development, the contributors recommend economic policy reform, establishment of more private enterprises, and encouragement of new domestic and foreign investment.

Ampah G. Johnson has been rector of the University of Benin and director of higher education in Togo. **Adeyemi O. Lawson** is president of the All-Africa Chambers of Commerce and is one of Nigeria's leading businesspeople.

Published in cooperation with Club d'Afrique and
the Center for International Private Enterprise

Growth, Equity, and Self-Reliance

Private Enterprise and African Economic Development

edited by
Ampah G. Johnson
and Adeyemi O. Lawson

Westview Press / Boulder and London

Westview Special Studies on Africa

This Westview softcover edition is printed on acid-free paper and bound in softcovers that carry the highest rating of the National Association of State Textbook Administrators, in consultation with the Association of American Publishers and the Book Manufacturers' Institute.

Figures 13.1 and 13.2 are reprinted by permission of *Economica,* the London School of Economics.

Published in 1987 in the United States of America by Westview Press, Inc.; Frederick A. Praeger, Publisher; 5500 Central Avenue, Boulder, Colorado 80301

Library of Congress Cataloging-in-Publication Data
Growth, equity, and self-reliance.
  (Westview special studies on Africa)
  1. Industry and state—Africa. 2. Africa—
Economic policy. 3. Laissez-faire.
I. Johnson, Ampah G. II. Lawson, Adeyemi O.
III. Series.
HD3616.A36G76 1987   338.96   87-14290
ISBN 0-8133-0486-5

Printed and bound in the United States of America

The paper used in this publication meets the requirements of the American National Standard for Permanence of Paper for Printed Library Materials Z39.48-1984.

6   5   4   3   2   1

Contents

Tables and Figures

Preface

Africa and its peoples provide fertile ground and tremendous energy for private economic initiatives. The potential, however, has not been realized.

What follows is a report on a conference that took this conviction as its point of departure. Held in Lomé, November 5–8, 1984, the conference provided a forum for African businesspeople, policymakers, and academics to discuss ways in which the African private sector can stimulate economic growth and development.

From a diverse group of people came a wide range of arguments and points of view. In addition to ten selected papers and addresses, this book includes an extensive overview section derived from tapes and workshop reports (Part 1). We have attempted to render synthetically the debate and dialogue of the participants and to do justice to the diversity of views, while emphasizing the underlying, recurrent points made in the conference. We have included appendixes containing a list of participants and the papers presented.

More people than can be named here deserve thanks for making the conference and this report possible. In particular, Millard Arnold, Anne Harrington, Ambassador Michael A. Samuels, Ambassador Owen D. Roberts, and Professor Yaovi Randolph rendered invaluable services ranging from constructive criticism to administrative energy to simple encouragement. Finally, James Fearon and Cheryl Whittaker May of the Center for International Private Enterprise (CIPE) were instrumental in the preparation of this final product.

Rector Ampah Johnson
Chief A. O. Lawson

1

Introduction: The Case for African Private Enterprise

On November 5, 1984, nearly 200 men and women from Africa, Europe, and the United States met in Lomé, Togo, to consider the following problem: How can private enterprise be promoted in Africa so as to foster economic growth and development? The participants—representing governments, universities, business and banking communities, and international organizations—contributed papers and thoughts in a series of ten workshops and three larger round table discussions. The four-day conference, organized by Club D'Afrique, was funded by the Center for International Private Enterprise (Washington, D.C.); the World Bank; the African Development Bank; the Federation of Chambers of Commerce, Industry, Agriculture, Mines, and Handicrafts of the Republic of Nigeria; the Chamber of Commerce, Industry, and Agriculture of the Republic of Togo; and several other African organizations.

The organizers designed the conference to serve as a catalyst for thinking about the role of private enterprise in Africa's economic development. In retrospect the conference appears to have served this purpose admirably. As a result of the Lomé initiative, several African governments and organizations have begun planning for conferences on similar or related themes. These conferences should further marshal and focus the ground swell of opinion in favor of economic liberalization and private enterprise solutions for Africa's future.

The participants came to Lomé from a hundred different backgrounds and with as many opinions and points of view regarding the conference topic: "Growth, Equity, and Self-Reliance: Private Enterprise in Africa—The Challenge of the 80's." Although in the end there was substantial agreement among the participants on the fundamental point that successful African economic development requires increased private initiative and enterprise, there was a tremendous diversity of views on the varied dimensions of the topic. The conference served as a forum for the open discussion and exchange of ideas about a relatively new policy course for African governments.

The organizers believe that a book reflecting on the proceedings of the conference and developing its principal themes can make a valuable contribution to the literature on the practice of private enterprise in Africa and provide direction to the policy dialogue that addresses the crucial issues of growth and development. The following arguments do not necessarily represent those of any individual participant of the Lomé conference; they are, rather, part of a mosaic that reflects the nature of the debate in Africa today.

Turning to Private Enterprise in Africa

Advocacy of economic liberalization and the bolstering of private enterprise in Africa is, of course, not entirely new. Analysts of all stripes have been offering suggestions, proposals, and reports with this intention for at least the last ten years. In the last five years, several widely read and noted reports have, in varying degrees and fashions, urged the adoption of more liberal import/export policies, pricing and taxation policies, the encouragement of private enterprise, and so on. There are fewer and fewer advocates of increased state intervention in African economies, nationalization of African industries, central economic planning, or protectionist trade policies.

Why? The severity of the present economic crisis in Africa and the almost universally pessimistic forecasts for Africa's future testify powerfully against the statist, interventionist policies followed by many African states since independence. African governments and the international community have watched in horror as the mass of African people slip deeper into poverty and ill health. According to the 1984 report of the African Development Bank and the Economic Commission on Africa, in the coming years Africa faces a nightmare. Most African economies appear to have prospects only for decline; many African governments are increasingly less able to carry out their basic functions, let alone implement a new policy.

The policies of the past appear bankrupt, and all know that something radically different must be done. But it cannot be said that the majority of African decisionmakers and intellectuals are enthusiastic and confident about the turn toward liberal economic policies. Often they are willing to follow the turn only because they see no viable alternative. And in some cases, it is not entirely a matter of choice. As debt-servicing demands increase and capacity to pay decreases, the influence of the World Bank and the International Monetary Fund (IMF) on the African governments' economic policies grows.

For a number of reasons, then, the turn toward a free enterprise system is being met, and will probably continue to be met, with suspicion, doubts, reluctance, and feelings of ambivalence. Under the circumstances of their introduction, liberal economic policies may be perceived by African governments as a default option or worse an unwelcome international imposition. Many Africans are further disposed against the private enterprise system for historical and cultural reasons.

None of this needs to be so. The positive case for the introduction of private enterprise systems in Africa is very strong. It simply needs to be made, with an eye kept on the particularities of African history, economy, and culture.

The Private Enterprise System in Africa: Theory and Practice

One important aim of the Lomé conference was to initiate discussion among African policymakers about the application of the theory of the private enterprise system. For historical reasons, many if not most Africans approach liberal economic models from a socialist perspective—via socialist critiques of liberal economic philosophy or via arguments about an indigenous African socialism. But to understand why a system is said to be bad is not necessarily to understand the theory and the strong points of the system itself.

Even given the intellectual climate prevailing in Africa since independence, it is rather surprising that more attention has not been paid to the relevance of classical liberal economic theory to contemporary Africa. In one crucial respect, state/society relations in Africa today resemble state/society relations in the eighteenth-century European nations Adam Smith studied. In neither situation was (or has) a real public/private sector distinction been fully articulated. In both eighteenth-century Europe and contemporary Africa it is hard to tell where the state ends and a private sector begins.

In *The Wealth of Nations* (1776), Smith gave the first comprehensive theoretical articulation of the private enterprise system. He proposed to discover the form of relationship between government and society most conducive to a nation's economic development. In Smith's view, a government can best encourage a nation's economic development by withdrawing its influence from markets and trade. In the context of his own society, he was arguing for the establishment of a politically and legally real distinction between public and private sectors. Like the majority of contemporary African economies, the economies of eighteenth-century Europe were organized in a hierarchical system of government-sanctioned monopolies. Individual persons, families, or companies were given legal right and state protection to exploit a particular internal market or a trade with foreign countries.

Why does such state involvement in markets stifle a nation's economic development? The underlying principle is well known. State-conferred monopolies restrict competition, and competition in a free market usually guarantees the most efficient production and allocation of scarce social resources. Smith, however, spoke of more than efficiency. He emphasized the benefits that accrue to society unexpectedly when individual producers are left to pursue their individual welfares without government interference or direction. One small industry leads to another and another after that as the process of the division of labor yields increasingly complex supply chains. Smith was amazed at how the market system leads to extensive economic diversification and interdependence—a linking of all producers in a durable network of exchange. This kind of "horizontal" economic interdependence is precisely what most African countries now lack.

Neither Smith nor the liberal economists of our age maintain that free markets everywhere and always guarantee optimal social results. Smith argued for government regulation of certain monopolies and government funding of public education, for example. Michael Roemer, an economist who has written on development in Africa, states that

> certain pervasive features, [called] "market imperfections," require government intervention: control of monopoly when it cannot be avoided; implementation of large investments that have substantial benefits external to the project itself, such as transportation, or power dams . . . ; regulation of activities that create external costs, such as pollution or the wasting of common, but limited resources like forests and fisheries; promotion of infant industries. Other intervention may be justified by national development goals that markets typically cannot achieve: measures to help disadvantaged groups, such as indigenous traders in East Africa, to catch up with advantaged ones, in this case, the Indian traders.[1]

Roemer goes on to observe that "the use of markets is not ideologically prescribed. It is, rather, one of the tools of public policy, and a very powerful one, that help guide the economy to achieve national goals" (p. 136). The importance of a healthy relationship between public and private sectors—one that generally ensures the independence of markets and trade—has been demonstrated repeatedly over the course of the last 200 years. High levels of production and growth within a large, complex national system are possible only if relatively free markets are used to allocate goods and stimulate production through the incentives of competition. The successful experiments of several socialist, Eastern-bloc countries with internal free markets bear this assertion out, as does China's recent policy change.

Too often, Smith's theory is understood atomistically. At the Lomé conference, for example, participants made such observations as "the market cannot do everything" or "the individualism required by the private enterprise system runs against the grain of African communal values." These caveats do not address the essence of the private enterprise system. The critical issue is the posture of government with respect to the national economy. The idea of a private enterprise system presumes the idea of a public/private distinction. The burden of effecting this distinction falls ultimately to the state because the state must guarantee the independence and autonomy of national markets and trade. (Certainly, groups in society may have a critical role in pressing for the establishment of a private enterprise system—see the section in Chapter 8 on business organizations.) There are thousands of enterprising people in contemporary Africa but very little private enterprise. Private enterprise does not exist until the political distinction is made real. Until then, the spirit of African enterprise is not harnessed to the national economy, to national development.

Throughout much of contemporary Africa, the public/private distinction exists only in theory, in the voice of an inherited legal system. In reality, most African states rest on patronage economies organized by tiers of monopoly. At the national level, parastatals monopolize the production and control the distribution of a vast range of commodities—beef, bottled beer, dairy products, shoes, textiles, foodstuffs. Below the parastatals, at the level of the smaller towns and countryside, powerful businesspeople with excellent state connections are often able to capture whole markets for themselves by obtaining exclusive distribution rights or by using political means to exclude competitors. Very often, the African entrepreneur's success depends on the ability to curry the favor of government—to obtain the requisite licenses, bypass prohibitive fees, and gain the political blessings of the regional "big man." Entrepreneurs succeed by pushing their way into and then entrenching themselves in the system of monopolies officially or unofficially sanctioned by the government. No government anywhere completely abstains from either formal or illicit involvement with business. However, in contemporary Africa the degree of political involvement in economics can blur the public/private sector distinction beyond recognition to the detriment of economic vitality. Not surprisingly, economic vitality in Africa is most often found in the informal sector, which often exists and flourishes in spite of the formal sector of public and (subsidized) private enterprise.

Certainly the parallel between the economies of eighteenth-century European states and the economies of present-day Africa should not be overdrawn. These two monopoly systems were born of different historical circumstances into different economic environments. The system of monopolies and crown corporations in eighteenth-century Europe was the legacy of feudalism, a system organized for the benefit of indigenous classes of nobles. By contrast, the monopoly system in Africa is the legacy of colonialism, a system organized for the benefit of foreign metropoles. The overwhelmingly external orientation of the African states' economies—what is sometimes called their extraversion—has worked against efforts to start a cycle of internal accumulation in the African states. Economic linkages extend vertically rather than horizontally; sectors of production depend not as much on each other as on inputs derived from foreign firms or parent companies.

Since independence, the policies of most African governments have done little to break the chain of monopolies that reaches from the marketing board to the protected subsidiary of a multinational corporation. In effect, African elites jumped into the chain, using import substitution and nationalization policies to create profitable monopoly enclaves in their new states.

In the early years of African independence, strong arguments could be made for import substitution strategies and extensive nationalization. Import substitution was regarded as an easy, practical means of industrializing. Demand for imported consumer goods such as shoes and clothes was already established; all the government had to do was protect fledgling domestic industries that would first assemble imported intermediate supplies and, in theory, progress to producing the whole product. A large public sector presence in the economy was viewed as a means of (1) replacing foreign capital while substituting for an as yet small or nonexistent indigenous private sector and (2) transferring technology to strategic economic sectors such as communications, transport, and some heavy industries. Many argued that given the low level of technical and managerial skills in most African populations at the time of independence, public enterprises could be important centers for apprenticeship and training in business skills. These are a few of the objective factors cited to buttress what was a very common ideological disposition favorable to state control and intervention.

Today, it is very hard to maintain these arguments. The annual growth of industrial production for the middle-income countries of sub-Saharan Africa fell from 17.7 percent for 1965 to 1973 to 1 percent for 1973 to 1983; the equivalent figures for the low-income countries are 6.9 and 0.6 percent.[2] As practiced in Africa, import substitution policies have succeeded in replacing consumer goods that were once imported but have failed to spur the growth of the intermediate and capital goods industries needed for genuine, self-sustaining industrialization. The sort of proliferation of interdependent, interlinked producers suggested by Adam Smith has not taken place, largely because of widespread effects of protection conferred on substitution industries. Quotas, import licensing, selective foreign exchange allocation, credit rationing, selective tariffs, price controls, and, most of all, overvalued currencies—all these devises commonly favor substitution industries with political clout over all other producers, farmers, manufacturers, and exporters most of all. Consumers, through high prices and poor selection, and governments, through subsidies given to loss-making parastatals, pay in the end for the inefficiency of protected, large-scale African industry.

The flip side of import substitution in Africa is extensive state involvement in directly productive activities. State-owned enterprises (SOEs) mushroomed in Africa after independence and now contribute an average of 20 percent to the gross domestic product (GDP). Average percent contribution to industrial GDP is much greater, possibly as high as 50 percent. The great majority of analyses of African SOEs have concluded that they are overextended and generally inefficient by standard economic criteria and constitute serious drains on government budgets. The tide has turned in favor of trimming back the public sector in Africa. A number of governments have begun the difficult but necessary process of parastatal reform.

The reasons given by analysts of the public sector for its poor performance fall generally into two categories: bad management and political/bureaucratic interference. The essential problem is that decisions within and without the public firm are not made according to profit/loss criteria but rather according to bureaucratic regulations or political rationales. Why? Because the boundary line between public and private is unclear. Nothing stops the minister from using the parastatal to employ hundreds of supporters; nothing stops the government from investing in a fruit juice production plant when there is no local market and no chance of producing competitively for export. A conference participant noted the case of the sugar mills built in the northern part of the Ivory Coast. Placed there to satisfy regional/ethnic political demands, they continue to produce at great cost to country's citizens—no sugar grows in the vicinity.

The point is that a monopoly of authority over economic decisions leads to wasteful decisions. We cannot even calculate the effects of public monopolies outside the government sphere, where other enterprises are suppressed.

The Strategy for Private Enterprise Growth in Africa

No theory is absolutely comprehensive and correct in all circumstances; to believe otherwise is to convert theory into dogma, thereby ruining one's ability to see clearly. Dogmatic overemphasis on the beauty of the free market mechanism can lead adherents to overlook crucial historical and political factors. Naturally, a well-articulated strategy will differ in its details from country to country and region to region. A basically simple theory may support a rather complex development strategy. The overview in Part 1 includes a discussion of the wide variety of components that may be incorporated in such a strategy.

The core of the theory must be broadly understood if a private enterprise development strategy is to have a good chance of success. Regardless of ideological orientation, all will agree that Africa's goal is the development of continental forces of production for the benefit of the African people—the heightened exploitation of Africa's natural resources for the sake of Africans. A nation's productive forces will develop as the number of producers working and trading within the national framework increases. To increase the level of production within the national framework governments must establish a healthy relationship between public and private sectors. To enlist the support of the greatest number of producers, governments must favor no one (or several) producers in particular. If through its policies a government thus ensures the autonomy of the markets within its bounds, the work of many entrepreneurs will build, from below, a thriving, highly interconnected national economy.

A development strategy based on private enterprise theory will necessarily have many components: trade policy, programs to aid new businesses with credit and technical assistance, macroeconomic policies that allow for optimal incentives and price structures, and so on. Participants at the Lomé conference focused on one key aspect of the private enterprise growth strategy, namely, the promotion of small and medium-sized enterprises (SMEs). Together with agriculture, SMEs are of central importance to any scenario of long-term development in Africa. SMEs are the means by which African states can overcome their economic "extraversion," their lack of internal, horizontal economic interdependence. An extensive network of SMEs implies a diversified economy capable of resisting and responding to external shocks. Beyond basic economic welfare, SMEs confer numerous other important social benefits. SMEs will often allocate resources more effectively and economically than large enterprises and generate more employment than large firms at lower cost per job. The more rapid spread of SMEs into poorer regions of developing countries can promote more equitable economic growth.

Other important elements of development strategy are treated here primarily as they relate to the situation of SMEs. Trade policy, privatization of parastatals, and government macro-economic policy are of interest here because they can affect the prospects for private initiative and SME growth. We certainly do not intend to downplay their importance. Even as it focused on the central issue of SMEs, the conference underscored the necessity of a climate favoring growth and development in Africa. A climate is total. Private enterprise promotion—and hence, economic development—depends on many factors that must be considered together in their totality. A climate for growth favors the efforts of private initiative from all sides.

The Lomé conference on private enterprise and development was a watershed in that it augurs a change of climate. For understandable reasons, business and private enterprise have not, in years past, had good names in Africa. They have been connected with exploitation and selfishness. For instance, in the late 1960s debate between Kenyan and Tanzanian leaders the Tanzanians proudly castigated Kenya for being a country where "man eats man"; in Tanzania, the Kenyans retorted, "man eats nothing."

The painful lesson of recent years is that man will "eat man" regardless. Whether he eats food and improves his standard of living is another matter. We hope this book will, however modestly, contribute to this latter end.

Notes

1. Michael Roemer, "Economic Development in Africa: Performance Since Independence, and a Strategy for the Future," *Daedalus* 3, no. 2 (spring 1982):136.

2. Statistics from *World Development Report 1985* (Washington, D.C.: World Bank, June 30, 1985), p. 176.

Part 1

Overview of the Conference

Introduction to Part 1

A lot of ground can be covered in a three-day conference. What follows is an overview of a very broad-ranging series of discussions. The Lomé conference was intended to help "get things going," to stimulate discussion of private enterprise alternatives for Africa's future. In this spirit, we set out in the following sections some of the basic arguments and more salient points made by the participants.

Each day's events began with a round table talk at which the parameters for the subsequent, more focused workshop discussions were fixed. The first round table, "Private Enterprise in the Development Process," introduced the subject and provided an opportunity for participants to essay the basic conceptual issues—the relative importance and capabilities of the public and private sectors, the causes of Africa's economic misfortune, and so on. The second round table, "Small and Medium-Sized Businesses as a Vehicle for Growth," provided an opportunity for a general discussion of the role of the African entrepreneur in promoting economic growth and suggested that small business development would be critical for the strengthening and diversification of Africa's economic base. The final round table, "Strategies for the Expansion of Markets and Trade," was concerned with the more long-term issue of structural change. Here the effects of various macroeconomic policy courses on the private sector were discussed, and, more generally, participants commented on the problem of how Africa should fit itself into the world economy.

2

Round Table 1: Private Enterprise in the Development Process

The ambivalence felt by many African intellectuals and policymakers toward the private enterprise system (or their conception of that system) came to the fore immediately during the first round table discussion. Although some participants argued that private enterprise could and should be the driving force behind economic growth on the continent, others felt that private enterprise, in accord with African traditions, should only complement state development planning and initiatives. This latter idea—that private enterprise might somehow be "un-African"—popped up again and again throughout the conference.

All agreed that the public sector had been overwhelmingly favored by African governments immediately after independence. As noted in Chapter 1, public enterprises became a central feature in the development strategies of most African countries, almost regardless of professed ideological orientation. In public enterprises, the newly independent regimes desired to affirm their political sovereignty, to counterbalance or offset large foreign economic presences, and to maximize the impact of their scarce capital resources by pooling them. Moreover, in the 1960s and early 1970s it was widely accepted that state enterprises could contribute to economic growth as effectively as the private sector, while checking bad social consequences of economic differentiation.

Participants who saw private enterprise playing a dynamic role in African development pointed to the economic ills that have resulted from interventionist, state-oriented policies. African countries as a group have the highest ratio of public expenditures to gross national product (GNP)—the state and its economic arms are monopolizing capital and credit that could be used more productively elsewhere. In the absence of the imperative of competition, corruption and mismanagement tend to go unchecked. Unrealistic exchange rates—exchange rates out of line with what the international currency market determines—and below-market prices for domestic agricultural produce have discouraged production for export and the expansion of domestic food production. Public sector waste and policies that have hamstrung the private sector have, in part, led to severe government revenue shortages and in turn to oppressively high debt burdens.

Participants on the other side argued that an adverse international economic environment, more than statist policies per se, had led to the present economic crisis. The strong emphasis on state hegemony and power, they observed, has to be seen against the colonial background, and further, in so far as it has meant an assertion of African cultural independence, the state focus has been a good thing. This argument was taken up and developed in the first workshop.

Workshop I: Historical, Social, and Cultural Obstacles to the Development of Private Enterprise

Papers by Elliot Skinner (United States), Comlan Aboki (Togo), and Kodjo Agbobli (Togo) outlined the colonial background to present-day African private enterprise (see Appendix A). Skinner observed that for several centuries before European colonization Africans had been increasingly drawn into trade with the Arabs of North Africa and the Gulf. The early nineteenth-century penetration of the British and French in West Africa aimed primarily at increasing the palm oil trade, but before long the European powers were actively inserting themselves into and commandeering preexisting trade circuits. The colonial powers developed the African economies as exporters of primary agricultural products—a process Agbobli called the "extraversion" of African economic structures. Development of local manufacturing and industry was prevented in all but the largest settler colonies, and in these latter countries the industry developed served settler markets and was managed and run by Europeans. Production and transport infrastructure served primary commodity exports alone; Skinner notes that "there were few attempts, outside the copper belt region of Central Africa, to have transportation systems cut across the colonies of different European powers. In most cases transportation arteries linked raw material production centers to the sea. Excellent roads petered out as they approached the borders of colonies belonging to different European powers." This pattern of development was bequeathed to the independent governments economies that were (and are) heavily dependent on the export of one or two primary commodities (cocoa, palm oil, coffee, tea, sisal). Export-to-GNP ratios of over 30 percent were not uncommon in Africa in 1960.

For the most part, the papers and discussion of the colonial legacy with regard to constraints on African private enterprise assumed that the extraversion of African economic structures constituted a serious obstacle to future private enterprise development. The implicit notion was that anything in any way "colonial" could not hold intended or unintended benefits for Africans. For example, Skinner, speaking of the process by which African peasant cultivators were enticed to shift to production of export crops by the prospect of imported manufactures, states, "the Africans [became] dependent upon European goods and felt constrained to pay the price for them." However, the phenomenal response of West (and where allowed, East) African peasant cultivators to the new opportunities for material prosperity opened up by the colonial pax and trade may also be seen as strong evidence that they are economically rational and capable agents. Furthermore, comparative analyses of other less developed countries (LDCs) have shown that a high level of involvement with the world economy is almost a sine qua non for the rapid economic growth of a small country. We will take up this point in more detail in the description of Workshop IX in this chapter.

Workshop I also focused on social and cultural obstacles to the development of African private enterprise. In papers given by Moustapha Kasse (Dakar), Iba der Thiam (Dakar), Genevieve Causse (Clermont-Ferrand), and Comlan Aboki (Togo), the argument that many African traditions are inimical to the Western economic system was forcefully articulated (see Appendix A). Kasse, Aboki, and Causse all saw an inevitable conflict between the demands of the entrepreneur's business and the demands of his or her extended family. The logic of personal relations that governs the one will not square with the impersonal logic that governs the other. In his paper Kasse argued that the "unwieldiness of the extended family, and of similar tribal and patriarchal systems of clientage constitutes a hard core of resistance to the emergence of modern forms of organization and production." Aboki, in his paper, ventured some thoughts on the nature of this core of resistance:

> The social environment for economic activity in Africa is characterized by personal relationships, which alone have the power to legitimate interactions. All relationships go back to personal relationships, and at the base of personal relationships one finds kinship relations. In this social context, the notions of demand, supply, efficiency, price, and profit are tinged by the subjectivity of personalization. It is sometimes difficult to distinguish between a client who is a legitimate buyer in the sense of classic capitalist theory, and a distant relative. Kinship relations un-

dergird economic relations. Even in urban society, the effects of traditional society emerge in the guise of ethnic solidarity associations and may constrain the development of [modern] economic activities.

The importance of relationships based of personal rather than contractual trust makes the institutionalization of a small enterprise difficult. In Aboki's words, "the length of the life of the enterprise . . . appears linked to the personal life of the entrepreneur"—the business dies with the owner because it has been erected around his personal relationships with employees, customers, and suppliers. Other cultures have solved this problem by instituting the family-run business, which is passed down from generation to generation. Except for scattered trading clans, this structure has not developed in force in Africa. Aboki attributes this to the problems caused by individual success in a deeply communal society and to the fickleness of the African entrepreneur's relatives.

For the African, the success of the enterprise is not always gauged by its profitability or its good management: rather, the entrepreneur must be armed with magic power capable of protecting him against his competitors; this dependence is expressed by occasional ceremonies to magic forces, by the adoption of a behavior (feeding, sexual, clothing, professional) which accentuates the moral hold that the traditional milieu has on him. . . . In Africa, a personal success is only tolerated as far as it profits the family or the village community. Moreover, for the entrepreneur who wants to protect himself against evil acts, it is best that he surround himself with members of his family; however the latter think less about the profitability of the enterprise than their own interests. . . . Social success is seen as a threat to social balance, it is thus fought through all means, if necessary by witchcraft and poisoning. This hostility, open or covert, contributes to creating an atmosphere of perpetual insecurity, fear and distrust of the entrepreneur.

Conference participants noted several other instances in which African cultural practices seemed to dampen entrepreneurial prospects and abilities. The practice of deference to elders may interfere with allocation of responsibilities according to skills and experience or may lead a small businessperson to employ excess workers to satisfy the demands of village gerontocrats. In his paper Causse said that African cultures have tended to give "priority to the distribution of economic wealth over its production." Finally, several participants noted that credit is often perceived differently in Africa than in the West—as a personal favor rather than as a loan with precise legal obligations attached.

Aboki suggested that profound modifications in social structure would
have to take place before a private enterprise–based system could really
take root in Africa. The success of capitalism in modern Japan, he
suggested, depended on modifications and adaptations of social structure induced under the Meiji regime of the late nineteenth century.
The idea that economic forms born in the West will have to be gradually,
arduously modified to fit the African reality was also discussed by Iba
der Thiam, Senegal's minister of national education.

In a provocative paper on the public/private distinction in Africa
(included in this volume as Chapter 7), Thiam locates the root of the
cultural obstacles to private enterprise in Africa in conflicting under-
standings of the nature of property. In the West, property is depersonalized—its value is abstracted and universalized in the form of a
money equivalent. By contrast,

> in precolonial black Africa among communal agricultural societies that
> were barely monetized, property does not appear to have had the same
> objective meaning. It was valued and exchanged less according to abstract
> economic laws than through a network of interpersonal social relation-
> ships; in terms of the identity and status of the partners involved;
> according to the norms of prestige and assistance; in the framework of
> an ethic based on the principle of the gift and countergift.
>
> Thus any property belonging to a traditional Wolof belonged and
> today still belongs to God, to the whole family, and to all the neighbors.
> To use it, the Wolof ran the risk (and today still runs the risk) of evoking
> harsh and pernicious criticism.

Thiam argued further that the precolonial African understanding of
property persists today in a substratum of belief and action. "I am
. . . convinced there exists an African type of economy, a type deeply
rooted in our past, which is still present according to its own modalities."

This African type of economy is characterized by the personalization
of property—"possession entails a whole series of obligations; therefore
the distinction between private and public is not as clear cut as it is
elsewhere." Thiam's argument is that because property in contemporary
Africa continues to have a communal rather than a wholly individual
significance, the public/private dichotomy as formulated in the West
cannot apply in the same manner. On this basis he concludes, "we
must proclaim the fundamental complementarity of the private and
public sectors; it is by this complementarity that Africa can achieve
self-sustaining development."

Thiam's argument is a coherent distillation and presentation of the
ambivalence that many Africans feel toward the private enterprise

system and the entrepreneur. Private enterprise is thought of as out of keeping with the African tradition of communalism. The notion of the individual or of property that is solely an individual's is understood as a threat to social harmony and welfare. The implication is that in the West the public and private sectors are not complementary but are rather somehow antagonistic.

Thiam is implicitly arguing that what once held for the African village grouping now holds, or should hold, for the African state. The state-level complementarity of public and private called for by Thiam has its precedent and ground in the still existing substratum of the African economy in which public and private mesh neatly together. Thiam seems to suggest that the modern African state intervenes in the economic affairs of its citizens according to an extension of cultural tradition and right. He would like to see the public and private sectors in Africa working together to promote economic development.

Thiam does not argue that the public/private distinction is invalid or illusory in the case of Africa. He recognizes that private initiative exists in Africa and that individual creativity and innovation are critical to the continent's development prospects. The ambivalence grows from a deeply felt worry that underlies Thiam's caveat on the public/private distinction in Africa; he is concerned that despite the importance of individual initiative the efforts of the individual in accumulating wealth will run against the interests of the whole group—that individual disposal of property is socially destructive. The passages previously quoted from Aboki and Thiam amply indicate how this concern emerges from an interpretation of African traditions. It may be presumed to have contributed to the generally negative attitudes of African governments to private enterprise and entrepreneurship over the past two and a half decades.

How can this dilemma be resolved? The real question is what "complementarity of public and private sectors" means. How can African public and private sectors work together most productively? Without doubt, the state in Africa will continue to play a large role in investment and action for economic development. The African state's historical momentum on this course is too great to stop outright; it would be absurd, simply in terms of what could realistically be accomplished, to advocate absolute laissez-faire for the sub-Saharan region. Nevertheless, because the state in Africa is so involved in the problem of economic development, the question of what is the best posture of the African state relative to the economy is all the more critical and urgent.

If the goal is economic progress—raising living standards by incorporating increasing numbers in a national network of production and trade—then what sort of complementarity leads to this end? It was argued in Chapter 1 that the state has the responsibility to create an environment conducive to economic growth and that the less it determines who should produce what, how, and where (in opposition to objective market conditions), the more likely rapid diversified economic growth will be. It is hard to see how the public sector is "complementing" the private sector if its policies are driving small entrepreneurs out of business and discouraging others from starting businesses.

As regards the perceived contradiction between African cultural traditions and business practice, the root problem is the almost subliminally held idea that the entrepreneur is doing social damage rather than social good when he or she organizes and runs a business for profit. But in the context of a modern state and economy, one who organizes a new means of production is contributing to the general welfare by using labor productively that was previously used less productively or not at all. In concrete terms, one who organizes a productive enterprise creates jobs and goods for consumers or other manufacturers and basically adds to everyone's income by tapping the labor potential of the population more fully.

The recent experience of Asia shows that social systems that emphasize the value of community as much as the value of the individual can adapt to, and prosper in, a modern competitive economic system. In Chapter 11, Paul W. Kuznets looks briefly at how Korean social structure and traditions have been adapted to contribute to private enterprise–oriented growth. At the grass roots level in Africa today, cultural resistance to the individual command of labor and property may inhibit the development of private enterprise and entrepreneurship. But contradictory tendencies exist in every culture: Many African traditions exalt individual achievement and individual command of wealth. The history of Africa going back before colonialism provides myriad examples of individual or family response to new economic incentives (e.g., palm oil production in West Africa). Over time, Africa will weave its cultural systems into modern economic arrangements. Furthermore, it is not possible that the resolution will be anything but a distinctly African resolution. The danger lies in elevating real or imagined elements of African tradition that are hostile to economic growth and development to the status of a state ideology.

Workshop II: Economic Obstacles to the Development of Private Enterprise

Three sorts of economic constraints were discussed in this workshop: (1) those pertaining to the size of African markets; (2) those pertaining to the structure of African markets; and (3) the problems suffered by the African private sector because of lack of access to capital and credit. These types of constraints are listed in order of their increasing susceptibility to planned change.

1. In the words of B. Y. Gu-Konu (Togo) (see Appendix A), African markets are "narrow" and "feeble." State population sizes in Africa are small relative to those in the rest of the world. Of the nineteen low-income countries listed by the World Bank with populations of less than 10 million, sixteen are African. Only five tropical African countries have populations greater than 20 million. Their market size is small not only in terms of numbers but more important in terms of what their populations have to spend. Per capita incomes are pitifully low in sub-Saharan Africa; very high population growth rates seem to doom future generations to similarly low standards of living.

2. The phrase "structure of African markets" refers to the manner in which demands for goods—consumer goods or inputs for other manufactures and industries—are satisfied. Several participants pointed out that the domination of multinationals and other foreign companies in an African country could shut out local entrepreneurs and suppress possibilities for the development of a diverse base of small businesses. State-sanctioned protective measures allow the larger companies (foreign owned, state owned, and private) to monopolize scarce foreign exchange and to benefit from favorable taxation, tariff, and licensing policies. African entrepreneurs are barred from producing to meet existing consumer demands by market monopolies bequeathed to parastatals, large foreign firms, and other protected large-scale ventures. The bureaucrats and politicians who control the licensing, taxing, and tariff policies profit at the expense of private sector and the general public.

One participant noted that it is not uncommon for more than 90 percent of the supplies to an African import-substituting industry to be imports. Import substitution as practiced in Africa has not promoted the development of indigenous supply manufactures but rather has generally replaced a dependence on imported consumer goods with an equal and in some countries greater dependence on imported capital goods. High levels of effective protection block out domestic suppliers and competitors. In his paper on multinationals and African private enterprise (Chapter 13 in this book), Bernard Kouassi weighs the good and bad effects of direct foreign investment for the development of indigenous enterprise.

3. African governments can do little about the size of their states or, in the short run, about the poverty of the majority of their citizens. They can do something fairly immediate about the policy structure that protects large industry and manufacturing at the expense of the growth of a diverse base of small manufactures and to the detriment

of their economic health in the long term. But at the same time, the structure of production in African countries will admit change only very slowly. The speed and nature of that change will depend heavily on the pace and pattern of investments made in Africa and on the availability and distribution of credit. The constraint on African entrepreneurship imposed by lack of access to credit and investment funds was explored in depth in Workshop III (see Chapter 3) but since it constitutes the most practical economic constraint on the development of African private enterprise, it drew some interesting comments in this workshop.

Mark Chona, a successful Zambian businessman, noted that the domination of large-scale enterprises in most African countries—domination often sanctioned and ensured by the state—hits small and medium-sized businesses hardest with respect to credit and foreign exchange allocations. Administratively determined, artificially low interest rates result in excess demand for credit, leading to credit rationing. The larger companies are best placed to take advantage of the rationing; they have the time and administrative resources to negotiate with the government and the banks. The same holds for foreign exchange allocations: It would be particularly desirable to spread them among efficient competitive producers because of the fundamental need of many African countries to stem declining export revenues. Permitting small exporters to retain a significant portion of their foreign exchange earnings allows them to increase and diversify their international trading.

Chona suggested that one good way of overcoming the protected preeminence of multinationals and state enterprises in African credit and exchange markets would be to require more joint ventures between foreign and indigenous enterprises and between large and small African enterprises. In part responding to this suggestion, Jim Thornton of the U.S.-based Joint Agricultural Consultative Committee observed that African governments needed to remember that they must compete for foreign investment with other countries in other parts of the world. To compete successfully, they have to establish policy and administrative environments that attract foreign investors—the investor has to see a return on an investment commensurate with the investment risk. He implied that African governments should not dissuade potential investors by overburdening them with regulations regarding how they should invest. Alexander Keyserlingk of the International Finance Corporation echoed Thornton's point. He thought it essential for African governments to realize that foreign investment is not charity; rather, it must be attracted by the prospect of a profit. He noted that his organization does not have the resources or the mandate to engage in small-business development. He argued that African governments and commercial banks should promote small businesses with favorable macroeconomic policies and programs for providing credit and technical assistance; by encouraging business expansion they enable more companies to reach the size at which it becomes reasonable for international investors to inject their funds and management experience.

Speaking about the problem of credit access for African small enterprises, economist Jeff Jackson also emphasized the role of government in establishing an atmosphere conducive to business growth. He cast the problem of credit access as a problem of financial flows. Investment capital has to be able to flow from sectors and regions with surpluses to those with a potential or actual demand. Governments can encourage small enterprise growth by strengthening and extending the operations of the financial sector into rural areas. Jackson argued that, for small enterprise development, price flexibility on the part of African governments is equally important. Administratively determined prices that do not correspond to real market prices inhibit smooth flows of capital from sectors with surpluses to sectors with growth potential.

3

Round Table 2: Small and Medium-Sized Businesses as a Vehicle for Growth

The African states, in varying degrees, presently lack a broad base of small and medium-sized enterprises. The manufacturing and industrial sector of an African country is typically divided into two segments. On the one hand, there is a large enterprise group composed of giant multinationals, state enterprises, and heavily protected and subsidized private industries. On the other, there is a mass of rural small-scale enterprises, often family run, involved in handicrafts and simple manufacturing. The two groups have very little to do with each other. Few forward or backward links tie them together. To generalize, most of the protected large enterprises in Africa perform the final assembly of imported supplies for consumer goods, which they sell largely to the urban "salariat." The highly competitive, largely rural, small enterprises use local resources to supply mainly rural consumers with simple, inexpensive products.

Since independence, many African governments have subsidized large industries and nonproductive public investments by taxing agriculture through state-run marketing boards and by indirectly taxing African consumers through the high prices they pay to support inefficient, protected large industry. In so far as the present economic crisis of Africa results from domestic policy inadequacies, these are its principal causes. Export agriculture and even food production in many countries have been driven out of official market channels by marketing board taxation, whereas the protection and subsidization directed toward large industry serve only to shore up inefficient, wasteful, often hopeless enterprises or to finance grand, unproductive public investments (e.g., state buildings), or simply to enrich corrupt politicians and administrators. Furthermore, the protection afforded to parastatals and other large industries effectively discourages the development of indigenous businesses that could compete with or supply the larger manufacturing sector.

Future economic prosperity for Africa demands, first, the reinvigoration of African agriculture and, second, efforts to put the large industrial, manufacturing, and service sector into a healthy, productive relationship with the rest of the economy. The account of Workshop VII (Agricultural and Private Initiative) given in Chapter 4, considers briefly the place of agriculture in the picture of private enterprise growth in Africa and several of the more important policy reforms and measures needed to stimulate farm production.

However, as we noted in Chapter 1, the main concern of the Lomé conference was not the development economics of African agriculture but the role of African small and medium-sized enterprises. Such enterprises are needed to bridge the divide between the large-scale, state-protected sector and the grass roots level of handicraft production and small manufacturers. A broad diverse base of African businesses could reduce the enclave nature of the present large manufacturing and service sector and bring it into a more productive relationship with the entire national economy. Small and medium-sized enterprises (SMEs) producing a variety of simple export products—simple food-processing industries seem to have ample potential in Africa—strengthen an economy against external shocks such as rapidly fluctuating commodity prices and give it more capacity to respond to long-term changes in terms of trade for primary goods.

The second round table afforded participants an opportunity to discuss the importance of developing SMEs in Africa and to raise the main problems involved in promoting such development. Participants noted that SMEs tend to use local production materials more than do large enterprises; that they can act as a labor-intensive alternative to state-run companies; that they are more suited than parastatals to agro-industry; that they are generally more competitive and efficient than parastatals and are able to admit failure sooner; and that in the long-run they can improve income distribution in a country.

However, though there was general agreement that SME growth must be encouraged in Africa, there were different views on how to go about encouraging it. Some participants tended to think in terms of direct state action to favor and promote individual or groups of small enterprises. others were more expressly concerned with setting the structural macroeconomic conditions that would encourage investment and entrepreneurial activity. Though discussed explicitly in Workshop IV, the role of African governments in allowing private enterprise-led growth was implicitly the subject of each workshop held on the second day of the conference.

Workshop III: Capital Access
and the Role of Financial Institutions

As noted in the discussion of Workshop II (Economic Constraints), the speed and nature of African economic change depend immediately on the pace and pattern of investments made in Africa and on the availability and distribution of credit. As the network and conduit for credit and investment, a country's financial system clearly plays a critical role here.

Participants emphasized two distinct capacities that African banking systems need to improve. First, they need an integrity and coverage that will draw the savings of the majority of rural customers and allow such savings to flow into productive investments. S. Sewa Lassey, a senior executive of Togo's Industrial and Commercial Bank, pointed out that the banking systems of most African countries are overwhelmingly oriented toward the cities and the savings of urban dwellers. In a paper (included in this volume as Chapter 14), Africa Club Secretary General Yaovi Randolph argues that "African banks must stop concentrating their main activities on real estate operations, where they stress the urban areas to the disadvantage of the rural areas, and favoring the big foreign companies to the detriment of African small and medium-sized enterprises." There is really no question but that institutional and legal biases against the penetration of the monetary system into the African countryside should be removed. The most important and prevalent are subsidized credit and the accompanying regulations concerning its allocation.

Second, participants stressed that African banks need to improve their capacity as creative credit providers. Many felt that the banks have shown very little flexibility or imagination in dealing with African enterprises. Often the same guarantee criteria applied to foreign multinationals are applied to new domestic enterprises, making it difficult or impossible for the latter to obtain a line of credit (see the example given by Kouassi in Chapter 13). From the comments of many participants, it would seem that banks in Africa rarely have the inclination or tools necessary to engage in creative financing of small and medium-sized enterprises. This is hardly surprising, as many of them came into being to serve the larger foreign and government creditors.

Admittedly, many of the tools required for small-enterprise development in Africa lie outside the scope of conventional bank services. John Moore, a U.S. entrepreneur working in Togo, noted that a sound business plan was essential both for the initial organization of a young African business and for obtaining loans from banks or other investors. He suggested that commercial banks and accounting firms in Africa could help prepare the business plans of new enterprises. Although this is a good idea, such undertakings would require large commitments of natural and human resources. The problem that continually comes up when discussing SME development in Africa is the cost and logistical difficulties involved. SMEs are hard to "reach" by their nature: They are numerous, geographically diffused, and undifferentiated. Further, the loan requirements of new businesses are often complex; it is always easier to finance a going concern. Businessman Stanley Cleveland delineated the several stages of a new business and the associated credit requirements, saying:

> From the point of view of new businesses in Togo, there is not one single need for financing but rather various needs throughout the 4–5 different stages of business development. (1) In starting a small business, an entrepreneur may see an opportunity but may not be sure how to translate the idea into action. Between $5,000 and $10,000 may be needed to carry an idea towards implementation. This is the feasibility study stage. (2) At the business plan stage, an entrepreneur needs to translate his concept into a more specific plan with a budget, a marketing plan, etc. Financial support is needed here, and especially assistance from an accountant. (3) At the capital investment stage, the entrepreneur must provide some of his or her own capital (so that he/she has a proven personal stake in the business) in order to enhance creditability. For long-term financing, commercial development banks or investors can provide capital. (4) When the new business is finally going, bank credit should be available to finance operational costs (such as inventory) which often place a heavy burden on any business.

As both Moore and Cleveland noted, loan costs are relatively higher for SMEs than for large enterprises. One participant put it bluntly: Commercial "banks are not designed to finance SMEs. This is not a new problem. The same issues were debated 15 to 16 years ago and will probably be debated 15 to 16 years from now. If we really want to help SMEs, we must focus more on [financial] structures, both national and international." A number of participants saw venture capital as a structure with great potential for aiding in the development of African SMEs; economist Jeff Jackson worked through this possibility in his presentation to the conference (Chapter 9).

Since the early 1970s there has been continual debate among economists and investors concerned with Africa over the question of capital access and bankable projects. Some argue that funds are available for worthy projects but few sound projects exist to invest in. Others argue that there are sound and bankable projects on the ground in Africa and that access to (as opposed to presence of) capital constitutes a major obstacle to their realization. Jackson takes the latter view, noting the successes of "shrewd operators" like Lonhro's Tiny Rowland, who are adept at spotting and developing projects that more conventional financiers would ignore in favor of larger, safer government-sponsored ventures. Venture capitalists can participate in the formulation of business plans, proposal development, and expansion possibilities. Jackson argues that because of their flexibility and company-specific nature, venture capital firms can provide the more informed, sophisticated approach to investment in Africa that SME development demands.

Workshop participants also stressed the need for more active constructive collaboration in investment activities by the major financial institutions concerned with Africa. There was general recognition that the present dire economic circumstances merit new approaches. As Jackson and Roland Ubogu point out in their chapters, Africa faces net capital outflows in the rest of the 1980s because of a sharp rise in payments on loans made in the late 1970s and because of a slacking of the pace of official development assistance. Clearly, African countries must make the best possible use of the capital they have or can obtain access to.

Several participants at Lomé, drawing back from the discussion of specific state or state-related actions to assist SME development, argued that the way to ensure the most efficient employment of the capital that Africa has at its disposal is to let a high proportion of domestic credit flow into the private rather than the public sector. Studies by economist Keith Marsden for the World Bank demonstrate a strong correlation between overall economic growth and the growth of domestic credit allowed to flow to the private sector. In a comparative analysis of seventeen African and Asian countries, he found that a

1% increase in the real rate of growth of private credit was associated with growth in GNP per head of 0.34%. The estimate is significant at the 99% confidence level. Economic growth was also positively related to the shares of private sector credit in total domestic credit and GNP. This suggests that the private sector used its financial resources more efficiently than the public sector. Countries which mobilized savings through financial intermediaries effectively, and ensured ample access to credit by the private sector over the twenty year period, achieved higher levels of gross domestic saving in relation to GNP. Saving ratios dropped sharply wherever governments came to dominate the demand for domestic credit. This was true for Africa as well as Asia. The differences among countries seem to be more related to differences in policy than to inherent characteristics of the two regions.[1]

When governments soak up available credit, the funds have often been used either for large unproductive public investments or to pay for political consolidation. In his analysis of the African debt crisis presented at Lomé (reprinted in this book as Chapter 8), Roland Ubogu of the University of Lagos emphasizes that the African governments will be able to manage their debts only if they allow productive, export-oriented industries to develop. This approach in turn requires more enlightened exchange rate and pricing policies. African governments mediate between outside investors and domestic business, and they set the parameters for the domestic banking and finance system. Any discussion of possibilities for future economic growth in Africa, whether private or public oriented, must invariably center on a discussion of government economic policy, which constitutes the locus for plannable change.

Workshop IV: **The Role of Governments**

Near the start of this workshop, Chief A. O. Lawson observed that "the role of African governments is the creation of conditions favorable to prosperity and economic growth." This proved to be a working statement on which all could agree.

But exactly what are "conditions favorable to prosperity and economic growth"? Two sorts of features may be identified. First, governments provide the institutional context for national economic activity. They must be stable and competently administered if the producers of society are to produce and exchange within the national economic framework. They must also evince a positive attitude toward the business community if trade and investment are to flourish. Second, the specific economic policies pursued by governments must encourage economic growth. Governments may set prices, interest rates, and exchange rates, tax businesses, consumers, exporters, and importers, and invest in infrastructure or their own enterprises. They can do all these things in ways that will either entice producers to work within the national system or gradually push them toward parallel market activity outside the official channels.

Almost every participant noted how critical political stability and peace are for African countries seeking to develop economically. In Uganda, Ethiopia, Angola, Mozambique, Ghana, and a number of countries, civil disorder has made economic progress impossible. Several participants also commented on the importance of consistent, evenhanded administration and policymaking within stable regimes. Jean-Dominique Lafay (Paris I) argued against the bad effects of frequent intervention by government leaders and bureaucracies in the affairs of the private sector. In the paper he presented at the conference (included in this book as Chapter 12), he argues that by their nature political leaders and state bureaucracies tend to work against the efficient resource allocation that comes about through the operation of competitive markets. Ruling politicians are concerned with staying in power (stability) and tend to use their power to distribute resources so as to shore themselves up. They generate revenues for distribution to supporters by forcing producers to work through administrative channels and thereby skim off "rents." Such behavior realigns business activities, depressing some and orienting others away from production and toward working to lower or circumvent the administrative rents. The same holds for the state bureaucracies, the basic goal of which, however, is expansion of size and control rather than stability. The argument is that government intervention in economic activity, when it subverts or bypasses market functioning, depresses growth while concentrating economic power in the hands of groups of admininstrators, politicians, and businesspeople. This is a strong theoretical argument for the adoption of liberal economic policies by contemporary African governments genuinely interested in helping to increase the per capita incomes of their citizens.

Several participants noted that African leadership groups have been excessively suspicious of their countries' private sectors, often seeing them as potential threats to their power. Despite the ministries or departments erected in many African countries with the avowed intention of promoting indigenous enterprise, these agencies often have little or no political clout and are commonly ineffective. One participant argued that specific ministerial actions to favor the private sector with such benefits as training programs will not be successful unless a macroeconomic policy environment conducive to entrepreneurship exists.

An excellent summary statement of the role of the state in promoting African private enterprise came from Boutros Boutros-Ghali, minister of state for foreign affairs of the Arab Republic of Egypt. It deserves to be quoted at length.

In Africa, the private sector is the peoples's sector; the field in which they show beyond doubt what they can do for themselves. Many are unaware how widespread the private sector is in Africa. In their minds, the private sector is large multinational corporations. But in Africa, it is family and cooperative farms, small merchants and entrepreneurs, ordinary people with ideas and initiative.

Many African communities have demonstrated that being poor or low income need not be a permanent constraint to development. Poor people will change long-standing behavioral patterns when presented with a real opportunity to improve their lives. This was clearly the case in the green revolution. Whole areas of the world, including Egypt within the African region, were introduced to new strains of wheat and rice which dramatically improved yields. Farmers were eager to apply the new seeds and production methods. When opportunity, price incentives and technology present themselves, people will take advantage of them.

In Africa, as elsewhere, economic development is a process of growth whose driving force resides in the entrepreneur, whether in industrial complexes, small farms or small business. The entrepreneur is motivated in his behavior by profit, using the most opportune combination of factors of production and having recourse to innovation. However, in a context such as that found today in most developing countries, a more incisive action is required from the state than that which was exercised by the state during the period of industrial take-off in many countries which are today developed. In this context, *the state cannot separate itself from the task of cooperating with the entrepreneur in priming development. But it should resist the temptation to become a protagonist and to eliminate the role of the entrepreneur, who is the driving force for development and innovation. The figure of the entrepreneur, private or semi-private, remains irreplaceable.*

The role of the state should focus on the creation of conditions favorable to entrepreneurship and innovation. In this context, the state and its central bank are called upon to foster the creation of institutions devoted to collecting household savings or those specialized in lending to agriculture, industry, housing, urban and rural cooperatives and small business. By improving and maintaining an adequate infrastructure, particularly in the transportation sector, the state could also remove some of the major constraints limiting private initiative.

Because of the sensitivity of private capital, clear statements are required from the state indicating the areas in which private investment, particularly foreign private investment, is considered desirable. The state would also promote private initiative and investment by providing appropriate legal frameworks for their encouragement. Expeditious approval procedures and consistency in policies relating to the private sector are essential in order to stimulate private initiative and investment. (Emphasis added.)

Workshop V: African Women and Private Initiative

Women make up a larger percentage of the total population in Africa than in other parts of the world, and they constitute the majority of marketplace workers. One participant estimated that 90 percent of marketplace activity is carried out by women. In West Africa in particular, trade is the prerogative and vocation of women.

Participants agreed that African women have not been allowed to play the role in SME development that they could play. First of all, there are legal and social obstacles. Throughout Africa women have few property rights; for this reason their enterprises are usually run at their husbands' discretion and sometimes direction. Social norms often sharply limit the bounds of a woman-run enterprise; it can only grow so large and can be involved in only a few acceptable activities. The obligation to take care of children and other relatives may also constrain potentially successful women entrepreneurs.

At this workshop Kokoe Andou Kuevidjen, an economic analyst for SITO (Lomé), presented a paper exploring the means by which African women's enterprises are financed and the ways such enterprises might be incorporated more productively in a national economy. She noted that traditionally African women were confined to two areas of commercial activity: trade in livestock and food products and trade in small imported manufactures. Today, however, African women are entering business in hairstyling, dressmaking, transportation, catering, confectionary, and hotel management. Kuevidjen's research revealed that the women entrepreneurs virtually always use the informal network to raise capital. However, these financing mechanisms are often formally articulated. If the woman entrepreneur cannot raise working capital through household savings of her own or from her husband, brothers, or other close relatives (the first options), she will often try local pawnbrokers or the local *tontine* network. The most common form of the tontine is a group of individuals who decide to pay a fixed amount every month into a common fund; each month one individual receives the sum collected. Tontines are common throughout Africa, but according to a paper on the subject presented by J. Michel Servet (Lyons), they are most popular in parts of West Africa where they have strong traditional roots. In Cameroon and Nigeria, it is not uncommon for a person to belong simultaneously to five or six tontines.

Kuevidjen pointed out that although these means of financing women's small businesses are sufficient for microenterprises, they are often not well suited for helping an enterprise expand beyond this level. For this purpose bank loans and/or credits are needed, and these are not often forthcoming to women's enterprises. Woman entrepreneurs tend not to have the educational skills needed to prepare business plans and to interact with the formal, modern sector banks. They often fear that involvement with any formal sector arm will mean taxation and harassment. On the other side, the banks and state development agencies are rarely geared toward or interested in financing women-run businesses. As a number of participants in this workshop observed, this is particularly unfortunate in regions where African women are working on hundreds of years of experience in trade. In West Africa there are many societies in which the women, more than the men, have the skills and drive needed to succeed in business development.

In her recommendations for improving the situation of African women entrepreneurs, Kuevidjen argued for the provision of training and credit facilities specifically for women in business. Such interventions, she thought, would be best made through women's associations. Some suggested that women's cooperatives for production and trade might be encouraged and supported by African governments. All agreed that governments should look into removing any existing legal barriers to formal women's enterprise.

Workshop VI: Business Organizations

"Business association" is an umbrella term for organizations such as chambers of commerce, employers' organizations, and other open groups of businesses formed to promote their collective interests (e.g., a chamber of mines and industry). As Michael Samuels (former executive director, Center for International Private Enterprise) noted in his remarks to the workshop participants, business organizations can play an especially important role in the development of African private enterprise.

The business community is an essential element in all policies—indeed as the productive and employment-creating element it can be justly termed the economic engine of all countries. As the representative of this social element, the effective business organization also represents the interests of society at large. If the private sector of a country suffers through lack of consideration or active discrimination by the government, all the citizens working and producing in the private sector suffer as well.

The ambivalence toward the private sector felt by many Africans reappeared in this workshop. Several participants argued that the private sector and its representatives had, first and foremost, to submit and conform their behavior to state-determined priorities. As several African businesspeople commented, this often translates to mean that the private sector is oppressed for the sake of the appreciation of government power and material resources.

The effective business organization is not created by the government in order to transmit or impose government policy on the national business community. Rather, it usually emerges from the business community, because the business community has its own collective needs and interests. Samuels pointed out that different elements of any business community will have both common and dissimilar needs and interests. Small businesses may need help with training programs in accounting, management, and technical subjects or information on markets and international trade, whereas big businesses might not. However, both small and large businesses need similar public policies on a number of important issues, and by teaming up in one organization they significantly increase their chances of being heard. Small businesses can use the financial support of big businesses; big businesses can use the numerical support of small businesses.

The principal commonality of a country's businesses is their interest in favorable, constructive government economic policies. It is against the interests of the majority of businesses in an industry if one or several are protected by exclusive tariff favors and exceptions; it is against the interests of the majority of businesses in an industry if price controls prevent them from meeting their costs (and consequently, market demand); it is against the interests of the majority of businesses in export industries if controlled, overvalued exchange rates make their products noncompetitive on the world market. In many African countries today, there are myriad examples of economic policies that favor politicians, bureaucrats, or individual businesses at the expense of the business community, and to a proportional extent, of the nation as a whole.

Samuels emphasized that an association is required to represent business interests. Individual businesspeople generally cannot afford to speak out for fear of government reprisal. "An association speaks the thoughts of many with one voice," allowing individuals to be absorbed anonymously in a group. Second, where business organizations are not organized in an association, powerful individual business interests will tend to dominate because of their influence in securing government favors, which can dampen the prospects of other businesses. This appears to be a particularly wide-spread problem in Africa, where the gap between large and small businesses is historically overlaid with very different levels of government intervention and protection and different business cultures. Samuels noted that while at present there are influential business persons in Africa, there are as yet few influential business communities.

The effective business association represents other collective business interests as well. The business community is most familiar with its human resource requirements and should be able to have input into the government's decisions on education.

Samuels stressed that African business associations had to keep their national character; they are not effective if they are extensions or instruments of foreign business enclaves. However, he noted with the concurrence of a number of workshop participants that a capable chamber of commerce can be a useful and attractive group for international organizations to work through. The World Bank and many other institutions would be highly receptive to an association that can act as a conduit for training that will have an indirect but clear effect on economic growth.

Most African business associations are regrettably weak and underdeveloped at present. The diverse forms of business associations inherited from colonial days or founded at independence have suffered equally diverse fates. Many have been co-opted and rendered ineffectual by jealous governments; many have fallen under the control of a single, powerful businessperson/politician (or a small group of them); many have withered as frequent regime changes or fiercely antibusiness policies have undermined them.

But some African business associations do function reasonably well; their example is especially relevant as more and more African countries turn to increasingly liberal, private enterprise–oriented policies. The comments of Gabriel Shamu, one of the directors of the Zimbabwe National Chamber of Commerce, are interesting in this regard. He described the Zimbabwe chamber as a force the government acknowledges; its advice is often sought on matters of policy that will affect the business community. It has conducted economic policy studies (for example, on the effects of government price and labor policies) and distributed them to important officials. The chamber's membership, which consists of both large and small companies, is provided with publications on relevant government legislation, taxation, and labor measures. Shamu feels that one of the key reasons for the Zimbabwe chamber's success is its strongly nonpolitical orientation: It does not take sides in factional political disputes; rather it confines itself to the role of liaison between the government and the private sector and acts to harmonize the interests of both.

Notes

1. Keith Marsden, "Private Enterprise Boosts Growth," *Journal of Economic Growth* 1, no. 1 (1986):17.

4

Round Table 3: Strategies for the Expansion of Markets and Trade

Should African countries adopt inward- or outward-looking trade policies, and what role should governments play in trade promotion? What sort of policies and/or government actions are needed to allow or foster a revitalization of African agriculture? How can African governments enable constructive industrial development?

The third round table shifted the focus of discussion from the agents of private enterprise themselves—chiefly, the small and medium-sized enterprises (SME) and the entrepreneur—to the general policy environment needed to encourage these agents. The role played by the private sector in a given country depends first on how policymakers answer these questions.

A country's or a continent's answers also imply a development strategy, an idea about the shape of future growth. Several participants at this round table chose to speak on the problem of how African economies could and should develop, given prevailing conditions in the world economy. They tended to emphasize schemes for intra-African institutional cooperation and collective solidarity against a hostile international environment.

The first speaker, Mohamed Hosney of Egypt's Ministry of Foreign Affairs, outlined the salient characteristics of the present economic crisis of Africa. He noted the sharp decline in terms of trade for African commodities since 1979, arguing that it had erased any domestic productivity gains made in the previous decade. He noted that African borrowers face very high interest rates, often 4 or 5 percent above the rates quoted to Western borrowers; thus African entrepreneurs and other investors must demonstrate very high rates of return (often 25 to 30 percent) on potential projects to attract financing. Capital flight to Europe and the United States is common across Africa. For these and other reasons, capital formation in Africa declined 6 percent from 1983 to 1984; as interest on large loans to private creditors made in the 1970s piles up, the continent faces net outflows of capital. In 1983, according to Hosney, the debt/export ratio of the African countries was an incredible 180 percent, reflecting both rapidly increasing indebtedness and continuing poor or worsened world prices for African commodities. Stabilization measures recommended by the IMF and/ or enacted by governments themselves have restricted the amount of credit flowing in African economies, limiting new private sector activity.

Hosney expressed the belief that only international cooperation and the united action by the African countries can turn Africa around economically. He saw a commodity stabilization program, administered by the UN Commission for Trade and Development, as a necessary step to enable widespread rapid economic growth on the continent.

Nigerian businessman Malingo Swinner offered a more practical proposal for the stabilization of African commodity prices. He reported his observations of the commodity exchanges in London and New York, where he witnessed firsthand the wild price fluctuations experienced by African products such as coffee, cocoa, soya, and tin in purely speculative trading. He argued that African countries could establish their own exchanges in their own countries—he noted plans for a Lagos exchange—perhaps giving African traders more influence in price determination.

A. Horton of the U.S.-based Opportunities Industrialization Center argued that Africa's recent economic crisis and the concomitant shift toward a heavier reliance on the private sector call for a rethinking of the role of the present framework of intra-African institutional cooperation. He suggested the creation of four continental authorities that would go beyond the Organization for African Unity (OAU), the African Development Bank (ADB), and the Economic Commission on Africa (ECA). He called for (1) a continental transport authority, which would raise capital and design and build roadways within Africa, to expand internal markets and open up internal trade possibilities; (2) an intracontinental communications authority, to help make it as easy to call from, say, Accra to Lagos as it is now to call from Lagos to London; this would greatly facilitate intra-African business; (3) a continental radio and television network, both to raise African self-consciousness and to better inform the rest of the world of what is happening and what is possible in Africa; and (4) the gradual creation of an African monetary union, starting with moves to make African currencies easily exchangeable and then progressing to the establishment of subregional currencies. Finally, Horton argued that Africa should plan an intracontinental division of labor, following the example of the United States (steel in Pittsburgh, wheat in the Midwest, movies in Hollywood, insurance in New Haven and Hartford).

These are exciting, if highly problematic, ideas. The concept of private enterprise implicit in these ideas is typical of that held by many participants and so deserves a brief comment. There is recognition that business development is necessary for African economic growth but at the same time a feeling that this development can and should be commanded or directed by supervisory institutions. Horton suggested that some high-level intra-African organization should plan a division of labors among the continent's varied states. Of course, the division of labor among the various states of the United States was not the result of any high-level planning but rather of comparative advantages and settlement patterns. Similarly, the establishment of subregional African currencies—a potentially good idea—will only become possible when more African governments adopt more liberal, flexible exchange rate policies, more in line with those that the international currency market establishes. Overvaluation may damage official intra-African trade even more than it hurts international trade, because smuggling is much more possible internally.

Trade and market expansion in Africa will naturally require the services of intra-African organizations like the OAU, the ADB, the ECA, and perhaps institutions similar to those proposed by Horton. However, the agricultural, industrial, and trade policies of individual states are the main determinants of economic and private enterprise growth in Africa today. These were the principal concerns of the workshops.

Workshop VII: **Agriculture and Private Initiative**

The failure of African agriculture in the 1970s and early 1980s is the most frightening component of what is referred to as the "African economic crisis." Although in the 1950s and 1960s agricultural production kept pace with or exceeded population growth, in the succeeding decades it fell behind across the continent; in a number of countries agricultural production actually declined. If African agriculture does not rebound to levels at least equal to those of population growth, the prospect of more widespread and severe famines in years to come increases. Presently, urban populations throughout Africa are being fed with grain imports and aid.

African agricultural productivity also must improve if any significant economic development is to occur in other sectors. Participants in the workshop noted four important relationships here: (1) Sluggish or declining agriculture has an immediately negative effect on rural incomes, which are important in determining the overall demand for nonfood goods; (2) agricultural processing and other agrobased industries need a steady and ample supply of raw materials; (3) a low level of agricultural production means fewer exported and more imported agricultural products and, therefore, less foreign exchange with which to purchase industrial and manufacturing input requirements; and (4) the health of agriculture critically affects the real price of food in the cities and thus affects the profitability of large-scale urban industry and all related urban goods and service production.

A number of reasons were cited explaining the poor performance of African agriculture: drought; population growth; war and political instability; neglect of agriculture by development planners; declining terms of trade in many of Africa's exported agricultural products; reliance in some areas on spectacularly inefficient state-sponsored collectives; inefficient input delivery systems and poor dissemination of new products and techniques; and finally, marketing systems, price policies, and exchange rate policies that have often discouraged rather than encouraged production.

This last factor—the incentive structure for small farmers—is very probably the determining factor. Much evidence indicates that given attractive prices and a reliable marketing system, the traditional African peasant will behave as classical economic theory would predict—as an economically rational agent. African countries that have maintained decent prices for farmers have not suffered the same declines in production as have those that have not: The Ivory Coast, Kenya, and Malawi compare favorably with Ghana, Tanzania, and Nigeria on this score.

Furthermore, as James Thornton of the Joint Agricultural Consultative Corporation (JACC) pointed out to workshop participants, low producer prices do more than depress food and export crop production; they also drain government revenues and force greater indebtedness.

> While governments can help reduce shocks of food price changes, most cannot afford to price large groups of foods below their cost. . . . When food prices are not directly related to producer prices, consumption is encouraged with no comparable stimulus for production. As a result, these policies become too costly to sustain, especially in cases where the subsidies come from borrowed funds.

Long-term subsidies for urban consumers, import substitution policies that lead to overvalued exchange rates and overpriced consumer goods, and other factors have gradually turned internal terms of trade against the African farmer. Discussing the Nigerian experience, Malingo

Swinner observed that the oil boom of the 1970s led the Nigerian governments to invest heavily in urban industry and in construction projects that were not income generating. He suggested that these investments had the effect of harming the agricultural sector. Studies of rates of return on capital investment across the continent in the 1970s seem to bear out Swinner's thinking. The World Bank's 1984 report on sub-Saharan Africa identified low return on (primarily urban, nonrevenue-producing) investments made in the 1970s as one of the principal determinants of declining per capita incomes.

Likewise many analysts have noted that the policies followed since independence in Africa have tended to favor industry to the detriment of agriculture. Marketing boards that should have been serving the best interests of farmers have instead been taken over and used by governments to appropriate funds for industrial development or simply to make politicians rich. The mechanism of appropriation is simple: The marketing boards and parastatals pay the farmers less than the world price for export crops or domestic natural price for food crops. In the short run this allows the boards to accumulate huge surpluses. In the long run it drives both food and cash crops out state channels; farmers shift from cash crops to food crops that they market, as best they can, through private technically illegal channels.

In general, the terms of the debate on African agriculture have shifted in recent years from emphasis on the administration of extension services and delivery systems to price policy and marketing systems. The former emphasis lends itself readily to a state-oriented, interventionist approach, and this attitude was represented at the workshop. One participant suggested that the concept of private action should be enlarged to include state initiatives in agricultural training and the provision of information, and so on. Though governments naturally have a role to play in agricultural development—some training and visitation programs for small farmers, for example—their role of ensuring the conditions that will stimulate production and encourage marketing through official or legal channels is probably more important.

The need for a constructive policy environment was thus the main focus of suggestions on how to improve agricultural productivity in the coming years, though many also suggested that more research on high-yielding crop varieties and more effective extension services would be required as well. Several participants focused their comments on how external agents could help. Jacques Bourinett (professor at the University of Aix-en-Provence) suggested that multilateral and bilateral donors should concentrate more on policy dialogue about agriculture and less on food relief; he noted that though food assistance may be absolutely necessary in the short term, it may in the long term be detrimental if it contributes to or allows the continuance of policies that penalize farmers.

Thornton of the JACC spoke on how non-African agents might participate in helping to turn African agriculture around. Since his remarks focus on the potential for private sector involvement in this process, they are quoted at length.

> Greater agricultural output in the developing world—and in the sub-Saharan African region in particular—will depend on accelerated development of the agricultural sector, an achievement requiring large amounts of capital, much of it having to be foreign and private. . . .

> Only the private sector can supply the volumes of capital, the management and the technologies required to successfully develop this sector, in my judgement. . . .

> Private sector investment in the agricultural sector must be encouraged. Yet, policies pursued by many developing countries not only have failed to emphasize agricultural development (many have actually constrained production), but they have not even created an environment conducive to growth and development of a viable private sector. Policy changes that create an attractive investment climate and encourage economic activity will be prerequisites to the development of these countries and their agricultural sectors in particular.

> I would like to mention a most effective technique now being increasingly employed to achieve large-scale agricultural production/marketing or production/processing/marketing objective, but which makes possible the involvement of thousands of private small family-farm enterprises. I refer to "nucleus" or "satellite" agribusiness enterprises that integrate the needed management, technical and marketing skills of larger companies with the investment, production and labor skills of small farmer owner-operators. Through such integrated systems thousands of small farmers can be afforded the opportunity to own and operate profitable farm enterprises. Such a system will provide them a buyer for their produce (the "core" or "nucleus" company) as well as provide them with the technical and other types of extension services they will require. These small farmers also should be able to obtain needed credit from existing financial institutions through presentation of forward contracts made with the "nucleus" company to purchase their products.

Workshop VIII: Light Manufacturing: Optimal Use of Skilled and Semiskilled Labor

Since the early 1960s, rapid industrial development has been a major preoccupation of African governments. The statistics on expansion of African industrial output in twenty-five years of independence are impressive. For the sub-Saharan region as a whole the contribution of industry to GDP increased from 17 to 27 percent between 1960 and 1982 (World Bank figures). But even so, African industry probably still constitutes less than 1 percent of world industrial output. The target of 2 percent by 2000 set by the UN Industrial Development Office is still a long way off, and given the present state of industry in Africa, it may be out of reach. Industrial growth rates plummeted in the 1970s and have shown no signs of recovery in the 1980s.

To date, African governments have focused on developing import-substituting consumer goods industries and in some countries heavy industries (steel plants, oil refineries). The focus of this workshop implicitly included the problems now encountered by these past efforts and pointed to a viable constructive means of developing African industry and manufacturing in the coming years.

The workshop allowed participants to analyze the role light industries can play in the economies of the African countries. The category of light industries includes textiles, clothing, pottery and similar wares, timber and other wood products, and most of all, agricultural processing. Such industries have three attractive features: They are relatively labor intensive, they employ local resources and skills, and they are readily directed to production for export.

These features are notably lacking in African industry as it has developed to date. In many African countries, import substitution policies have worked against a healthy sustained development of industry and manufacturing. Constant high levels of protection for import-substituting industries and related overvalued exchange rates have created strong disincentives for would-be domestic producers of inputs for domestic industries and for export processing industries of all kinds (agricultural and manufacturing). In effect, because of protection policies that let industries stay in their infant stage, African countries have simply switched from a dependence on consumer goods imports (in the 1950s) to a dependence on imported capital and intermediate goods (today). The economic shocks incurred in the 1970s and the international recession of recent years have made it painfully clear that inefficient import substitution can no longer be sustained. Consumers pay for the inefficiency allowed by high protection through inflated domestic prices and a poor selection of manufactured goods; governments pay by subsidizing inefficient state-owned enterprises, which are sometimes losing money because of government pricing policies; potential exporters, who could be earning the essential foreign exchange, pay through overvalued exchange rates, which keep prices of imported capital goods for the substitution industries artificially low while forcing the prices of exports artificially high for international buyers.

Many African governments have also demonstrated a disregard of comparative advantage, investing in large-scale capital-intensive industries, sometimes in sectors not at all suited to present economic and social conditions in Africa (steel, oil, chemicals). In many countries, the philosophy that "any smokestack is a good smokestack" has prevailed among government planners. In general, the policies favoring import substitution have encouraged more capital-intensive technologies than are optimally efficient. Subsidized credit for modern-sector manufacturers, a nearly universal feature of government policies in Africa, may also have contributed to investment in inappropriately capital-intensive industry.

Labor-intensive light industries provide an avenue of employment for unskilled labor and thus an avenue for the development of a more skilled labor force. Because light industries are more apt to be located in the countryside or at least outside the major urban centers, they may help slow rural-urban migration as well. Participants in the workshop stressed the possibilities of light industries oriented toward export processing; the Asian example was clearly very much on their minds. Several successful experiments with letting private African businesspeople retain a portion of their foreign exchange earnings were noted; this practice stimulates further investment in export activity and tends to promote more efficient allocation of investments than state planners have been capable of.

Suggestions for means of promoting light industry in Africa were of two kinds. First, some argued that the principal obstacle has been the policy of high protection for substitution industries, which discourages exporting and the growth of indigenous supply manufacturers. Although capital access and access to training in modern business methods are important, small-scale enterprise in most African countries would be best served by policy changes that reduce the enclave nature of African industry. Abolition of quotas, automaticity in foreign exchange allocation, open licensing for imports and exports, elimination of extensive price controls, and market-determined interest rates would probably favor the growth of African light industry more than any other changes.

Second, a number of participants stressed the role of foreign investment in the promotion of light industry. Some argued that up to 100 percent foreign ownership should be allowed in a new industrial venture in Africa because capital, technology, and managerial skills are so scarce in many countries. In many African countries, there will be deep and difficult political obstacles to open policies with regard to foreign investment. Certain compromise patterns may be devised; several participants mentioned the option of the state leasing management responsibilities to foreign groups. This is known as the *contrat* plan in francophone Africa and appears to have had some success.

Workshop IX: Technology Transfer

To a large extent, rapid growth in developing countries is made possible by the adoption of technologies that increase productivity. This workshop focused on the question of technology transfer in the African context. Several participants noted that many past efforts at technology transfer to Africa had failed because of unrealistic planning by state agencies. Many technologies inappropriate to the conditions in Africa have been acquired; either intended users lacked the knowledge and means to use and keep up the productivity increasing equipment or the imported technologies have simply been noneconomic, given local production systems and factor proportions.

The question then is how African states can ensure that imported technology will be absorbable and usable. A number of strategies were suggested, most focusing on ways in which the private sector's role in deleting technology requirements can be increased. Joint ventures, regional associations of like businesses, and improved public facilities for the dissemination of information about technology were all discussed. The bottom line, aptly summarized by Fogan Sossah of the Togo Chamber of Commerce, was that "markets would better determine the acquisition and utilization of appropriate technology" than state planning agencies because "bankruptcy is the immediate sanction against the private sector."

Stanley Straughter, a private financial consultant from the United States, gave an interesting presentation on a means for the dissemination of new technologies and methods among small business in the United States. He discussed the model of business service centers, a program funded by public and private sources. Straughter pointed out that, contrary to what we might think about the success of U.S. businesses, small and minority-owned businesses are having difficulty in the areas of growth and competitiveness. Government programs, though showing some success, have not had the expected impact.

These business service centers (BSCs) are staffed by professionals in accounting, finance, management, and marketing. Although most are privately run, some BSCs are run by universities. Another element of the BSC program is the Technology Commercialization Program. Technology commercialization centers (TCCs), run by universities, serve two functions. First, they help small businesspeople evaluate the commercial potential of a new product or innovation and, if necessary, acquire patent protection. Second, the TCCs are given access to prod-

ucts developed by government labs or research facilities. Any unclassified development is available for development and cannot be patented.
  BSCs provide the following services:

Finance

Financial plan
Loan/investment package
Tax advisory and planning
Mergers and acquisitions

Management

Staff and personnel review
Accounting and administrative systems

Marketing

Market reseach
Market development
Procurement and brokering

Exporting

Exporting
Market identification

In summary, there was agreement on the fact that technology must be transferred into Africa because Africa's scientific and technical sector is embryonic and the greatest proportion of research and development occurs in the developed nations.

Workshop X: Development Strategies

Throughout the conference and particularly in this workshop, participants repeatedly expressed a deep feeling of discontent with Africa's present place in the world economy. Africans cannot be the "hewers of wood and drawers of water" for the rest of the world forever. The question is how to escape from this position.

At the start of the final workshop, Jean Austruy of the University of Paris noted that the industrialized countries had each followed distinct paths of economic growth, appropriate to, or constrained by, their particular circumstances, institutions, and traditions. The African countries too, he suggested, would have to find their own distinct development paths.

Given the African countries economic circumstances, institutions, and traditions, what sort of paths should these be? Dependency theory, as developed by Latin American scholars and adapted by African academics such as Samir Amin and Walter Rodney, has been influential among African policymakers and academics; it has inclined many toward various brands of economic isolationism. The theory that the developed countries profit disproportionately from all interactions with the underdeveloped countries—whereas the underdeveloped countries either profit negligibly or actually lose out—implies that it is in the best interests of the underdeveloped countries to disconnect themselves from the world economy. The often-heard call for collective self-reliance of African states echoes this sentiment, though it does not necessarily imply isolationism.

The abuses of multinationals, the apparent unfairness of the world commodity trade, First World protectionism, developed country monopolies in market information and technology—these and other features of Africa's international environment seem to support the claim that the international economic system generally is unrelentingly unfavorable to the poorest countries. A few years ago, this argument would not have met strong opposition in any quarter. But the argument is increasingly hard to maintain in light of the comparative experience of countries with open and closed economies in the past years. Small countries that have pursued isolationist courses have not done well economically. In contrasts, the East Asian Gang of Four (Hong Kong, Singapore, South Korea, and Taiwan) have demonstrated the potentially phenomenal results of growth that stem from an emphasis on private initiative in exports. Even in Africa, the countries that have grown fastest economically are for the most part those whose governments have encouraged (or at least, not discouraged) export activity by private agents—the Ivory Coast, Kenya, Zimbabwe, and Malawi compare favorably with, say, Ghana, Tanzania, and Guinea (until recently).

Paul Kuznets of Indiana University presented a paper on private initiative in the development experience of South Korea, as a case study to be considered by African policymakers (included in this volume as Chapter 11). Several key points deserve comment here. First, Kuznets notes that the Korean government's spending as a percent of GDP is small relative to international averages and is considerably less than for the African countries. The same holds for Korea's state-owned enterprises (SOEs): "Shares of SOEs in GDP were somewhat below the 10 percent average for developing countries in 1980 and well below SOE shares in Zambia, Ghana, Guinea, Tanzania, Togo, and the Ivory Coast." His analysis "indicates that a government's size is influenced by political preference and that Korea's relatively small public sector is the byproduct of a political philosophy that emphasizes output expansion rather than social goals." Thus he suggests that there is a rough inverse correlation between size of government and its participation in productive activity, on the one hand, and scope for private initiative and economic growth, on the other.

Second, while noting significant instances of government intervention in the Korean economy, Kuznets connects the amazing takeoff of Korea to changes made by the Park regime in 1961, changes marked "by devaluation, import liberalization, a general relaxation of controls, and a series of measures designed to expand exports." Of the three sorts of government intervention he considers—planning, credit allocation, and export promotion measures—only the export promotion measures are judged to have had an unequivocably favorable effect on scope for private initiative and GNP growth. Interestingly for African states, government rationing of credit is argued to restrict the total amount of credit available and, in all likelihood, to favor the concentration of economic power in the hands of few very large firms (the *chaebol*). This is good demonstration of how administrative circumvention of the market mechanism can lead to rationing and rents, which have the adverse effects of slowing economic growth while concentrating its benefits (see also Chapter 12).

On the other hand, Kuznets notes that government intervention to promote exports has had very significant beneficial effects on Korean growth. Some of these measures might be usefully and profitably considered by African governments. Tying import credits to exports, granting tax exemptions for increased exports, and most important, linking credit access to export success are tested possibilities.

In effect, Kuznets argues, the Korean government's interventions in export promotion offset the effects of "the market distortion created by the import controls used to protect fledgling import substitution industries. Export promotion has therefore redirected private initiative from profiting by protection or by avoiding import controls to profiting by export production."

This example is especially relevant for present-day African governments. The point is that successful government interventions are those that improve, rather than bypass or subvert, market functioning. Ideally, the Korean government might have gradually removed protective measures for substitution industries while reducing disincentives to export. The second best solution—intervening to favor exports relative to production for the domestic market—has proved successful itself, however, thus supporting the argument that international trade is a small country's best bet for rapid economic development.

A collective self-reliance that means greatly expanded intra-African trade is obviously a valid and important goal for African countries. The workshop discussion that followed the presentation of Kuznets' paper suggested that such a collective self-reliance may depend on the economic success of outward-looking trade policies pursued by individual African states. Internal infrastructure must be paid for, and there must be a rising demand for goods within Africa. Both these conditions for a collective self-reliance presume rising national incomes, which may be most rapidly brought about by encouraging private agents to develop export trade.

Part 2

Selected Conference Materials

5

Opening Address

Chief Adeyemi Olusola Lawson
Chairman of the Colloquium

In Africa we are unhappily far below the level of development we would wish! More than two decades after most of our countries achieved political independence, we still have the greatest concentration of the poorest countries of the world in our corner of the globe. We still feel obliged to cry out and demand that the dignity of the African as a human being has to be generally and naturally acknowledged. We have not yet succeeded in earning that acknowledgment and respect as a right. Let us note that I have deliberately used an expression which underlines our responsibility for earning and not just demanding that acknowledgment and respect.

It is in this appreciation that I welcome the opportunity, the theme, and the stated objectives of this colloquium as a potentially valuable contribution in the process of finding solutions to some of the most important and pressing needs of Africa today.

How do we ensure such economic emancipation as will enable us to chart and control our own course for real development and growth? How do we create an environment which makes for justifiable pride in Africa and take our proper position in the community of nations and among humanity, naturally and unquestionably acknowledged as an equal because we have proved it and earned it?

"Growth, Equity and Self-Reliance: Private Initiative in Africa—the Challenge of the 80's." This theme invites us to focus our gaze on the economic future of Africa in general and the role of private initiative with its challenges in the 1980s in particular.

Entrepreneurship is a key factor in the development process. The entrepreneur demonstrates a capacity for innovation, risk-bearing, and an ability to seek investments, new markets, products, and technology.

Many of our countries in Africa harbor a sizable private sector. Even where these fields of operation may yet be comparatively humble, these can soon be enhanced by appropriate stimulation. Even where there is a scarcity of entrepreneurial resources, their increase can be promoted by economic stimuli and incentives. Unfortunately, while enlightened economic planners see the private sector as a premier mobile of development, many public sector functionaries in Africa permit its existence under sufferance. The erstwhile colonial phobia creates a fear of private enterprise as if it were an instrument of exploitation. Policymakers therefore lean further and further away from healthy regulation of private enterprise toward the extreme of completely rejecting this proven and necessary partner in development.

The role of private enterprise as an engine of growth is the key to affluence in any nation. For evidence, one need only examine the various economies of the world. In the several corners of the globe where the role of private initiative is not properly acknowledged in the system, real affluence appears to be elusive. It is difficult to achieve the highest levels of efficiency in an economic system without competition and the sanctions of open markets.

It is not for me to preempt the work which will be turned out from the several workshops that will be dealing with the theme of this conference. However, my experience and exposure in the market place and observations of the attitude of the public sector in many countries of Africa to private enterprise oblige me to draw some attention to the great need in Africa for responsible policymakers to be advised on the need for identifying, as their necessary partners in progress, the economic agents of the private sector. Our human resources, particularly in entrepreneurial talents, should always be harnessed for the good of all and for the development and growth of our national economies.

If political decisions in Africa are always conscious of the need to maintain an atmosphere conducive to the healthy contribution to economic growth made by private initiative, a gate will have been opened for the inflow of this contribution that would substantially enhance the development of our many nations and economies.

On our part, as private economic agents, we share the desire for, and appreciation of, the many incentives which make for successful private sector operations. Nonetheless, there is no doubt that in Africa today the private sector agent is obliged to be more conscious of the need for his activities to be guided by the overriding demands of patriotism and loyalty to the interests of Africa, and to the government and people of his country. He should be a proud and humble contributor to the welfare and happiness of the people of his lands.

There is a need for an increasingly higher level of discipline in the management of our private lives, and in the administration of our affairs in government and in business. If we in Africa can today take a hard look at ourselves in the mirror, we shall find a number of blemishes which only a more applied sense of discipline can help remove. Whether we work in the private or public sector, we must always be conscious of a need for great efficiency in the management of resources. This calls not only for experience and know-how, but also discipline.

In the world today, tactfully subdued, but critical voices are calling Africans to demonstrate initiative and capability in the management of their own affairs and the solution of their own problems. For too long we have permitted ourselves the paralyzing delusion that most of our problems are consequent upon our colonial past. We overlook the fact that there are other nations in the world which were colonized, but have with disciplined strides progressed toward emergence as developed economies. There are also, conversely, countries which have never been colonized and yet remain backward and undeveloped because there is lack of the requisite level of discipline in the planning and management of their affairs.

Together with an improved and high level of discipline, I would like to see the emergence of Commissions for Economic Growth at national, regional, and other levels in Africa. Such commissions would ensure the private economic agent a voice in the formulation of the economic programs of his country. His experience should be increasingly born of exposure, not only to his national market place, but to international markets. Such experience can then be harnessed to make a worthy contribution to economic growth.

Finally, Your Excellency, Professor Ampah Johnson, distinguished ladies and gentlemen, let me express with humble gratitude my thanks for the opportunity to participate in this colloquium and to express the hope that the recommendations turned out from our several workshops this week will be well and thoroughly considered, and that they will serve as meaningful contributions to the planning of strategies for economic growth and development.

I thank you all.

6

Plenary Session Address

Michael A. Samuels

Executive Director,
Center for International Private Enterprise

The last decade has not been a happy one for the African economic scene. Development efforts have stagnated, political difficulties have been widespread, and population has continued to grow rapidly. In many countries, the gross national product has been low or negative. In many, the gross national product per capita has actually declined.

No one can be happy about this situation. This conference is directed at attempting to seek new solutions out of this sad situation. What I'd like to share with you is not a specific answer; I have no specific answer. I would like to share with you first a vision, a vantage point for looking at the problems, and then examine areas where solutions may be found. My honest belief is that the problems of growth and development in Africa are solvable. That is the very message of this conference.

Societies grow economically—not because of their political leaders, but because of the efforts of the citizens. In fact, actions by political leaders often inhibit economic growth through venality, bad policies, inaction, lack of understanding, and more. The challenge before Africa today is how to stimulate and sustain economic growth, often in spite of political leaders. I say this to you because, after all, this is a conference not primarily with political dimensions but rather with economic ones.

We all share the view that it is our goal to encourage a better life for all citizens. By a better life, I mean health, peace, and wealth, and all that those three things in combination may bring with them. The premise of my presentation is that the keystone to this better life is economic growth. And the keystone to economic growth is to free up the spirit and efforts of people so that they can contribute to their own economic growth.

For a variety of reasons that I won't go into here because they will be discussed more fully in later sessions, during the last two decades, much of Africa has been caught up with a variety of ideologies: anticolonial, prosocialist, antisocialist, and several others. They have often been reactive, rather than prescriptive. The economic implications have usually been secondary to political necessities. Much of Africa has agreed too easily to Kwame Nkrumah's plea first to gain the "political kingdom." We know now that, in contrast to his prediction, "all else" has not followed in the wake of that political power. Power has been exercised, but often not in ways that have been effective for economic growth.

The ideologies of other continents and societies can not be transferred in whole to Africa. Socialism, communism, or capitalism—none of these provides an African framework. Such a framework will evolve from both the experiences elsewhere and those in Africa. But there needs to be agreement on the fundamentals. First, it is necessary to accept the fact that there exists a state and that the state does have a role that relates to all matters within its borders, especially the economic environment. But, at the same time, it is necessary to realize that the state cannot be an efficient producer of wealth. The state is not the mechanism best suited to make efficient decisions, and the state is not able to force its citizens to work, to innovate, to save, and to invest. Such behavior—participation and drive of citizens (if you wish, call them "the masses")—is the key for economic growth.

I have made these comments in order to provide an introduction to sketching two levels that I believe should provide the framework for the deliberations of this conference. The first level is a plea for understanding—understanding that the goal must be greater involvement and more productive activities of more people, not of their institutions and not of their leaders, and not of their governments, but rather of the people themselves. The second level is the search for mechanisms to bring about this participation. I'd like now to discuss a little bit my views on each one of these matters.

First, the need to involve the people. Some people believe that economic planning is absolutely necessary. Some believe that it is useless. I believe that the truth is somewhere in between. Plans are good and necessary for any institution. Rigidity, however, is bad. Government must seek ways to free up the spirit of its people, to allow for spontaneity of action and energies, to encourage the kind of serendipity that brings about geometric economic growth. What government needs to consider, and what many of you in this conference need to consider, is something that may be new to you. There is a need to learn how to unleash the people and their creativity, how to channel actions into productive activities, and how to encourage greater participation, greater accumulation of wealth, and greater investment of wealth.

Now part of the problem is that, in the eyes of some, the accumulation of wealth is bad rather than good. In the eyes of those who have accumulated it, the investment of wealth may be dangerous rather than secure. And in the eyes of many, those who have accumulated have done so corruptly and those who have invested have done so foolishly. As long as these views are held, the economies of Africa will suffer. Many in Africa need to reconsider their views of the private sector and realize that it is a constructive vehicle for growth. The major playing field for these activities is the marketplace, the locale for economic activity.

The most dramatic recent testimony to the failure of ignoring the dynamic potential of market economics took place last month. The People's Republic of China unveiled bold changes in its economic policies. It discarded tight state controls and broad state planning. Instead, it freed a large portion of the economy, freed prices, and gave autonomy for most factories. Finally, it recognized that only when some individuals are allowed and encouraged to get better off first through diligent work will more and more people be prompted to take the road of prosperity.

Just as this can happen in China, so, too, can it happen in Africa.

Think back to precolonial times. There was a private sector, it was dynamic, and it was effective. Whether it was the trader or the blacksmith or the transporter, this was where dynamism occurred. I realize the existence of a social security system of family ties and ethnic ties, and I realize the extent to which this is often a vehicle of welfare rather than growth. This is a problem with which Africa must contend. Nevertheless, the spirit of enterprise is not foreign to Africa; it is, in fact, indigenous to Africa. Go to any marketplace and you will see it.

In certain parts of the continent, it became fashionable in the 1960s to talk about self-reliance. This is a very important concept. But it is important to examine what it has brought about and what it could bring about. A self-reliance that shuts out the world's marketplace, that closes opportunities for a country in the world around it, and that dictates to the people from the capital what they should be doing and what is best for them is a collectivism that is a sure recipe for failure. A self-reliance that encourages rather than discourages, that provides opportunity rather than dampens it, is what ought to be the goal. To provide such opportunity within a growing world trade system is also of great importance.

Self-reliance also carries with it an appropriate concern for equity. Equity of what? Opportunity? Equal salaries? Equal wealth? I'm not sure that this is a useful definition of equity. Some people will work harder than others and should be rewarded for so working. Some will accumulate, and others will spend. Some will put their savings into productive uses (investments), and others will put their savings underneath the mattress not allowing them to be productive for the society. Some will keep their capital, their savings, in their own country, and others will send it to Switzerland or other safe havens. Those who do the latter do not help their own country. But very few African governments have provided the atmosphere that would encourage savings, investment, and maintaining working capital in their own economies.

To establish this growth-oriented economic atmosphere is the major challenge of Africa today.

Unfortunately, largely in the context of the colonial period, a historical pattern developed in much of Africa. It is a pattern of looking for help from outside. Some political scientists call this "dependency." Perhaps it was this pattern that Julius Nyerere tried to break in his calls for self-reliance. In that context, self-reliance does make some sense. The feeling of impotence in the world's economic scene has led many leaders of developing countries to make unrealistic calls for a New International Economic Order and to call for an international redistribution of wealth. They have failed to realize that their internal policies have been a major factor. The industrialized countries are not prepared to "share" their portions. The effective developing countries, however, will increase their own portions, as has been particularly true in Asia over the last decade.

Dependency has not only been a factor between nations. It has also been found within a nation's borders. People in the rural areas have often looked to the cities for help as well. Meanwhile, actions in the cities have frequently been counterproductive to growth. In fact, many urban-oriented policies are primarily political or welfare related; rarely are they growth oriented. There have been no more devastating policies in Africa than those related to agriculture.

By maintaining producer prices low in order to subsidize urban consumers, African governments have discouraged farming and food production. By controlling prices of food at low levels, African governments have ignored market forces, seen a reduction in agricultural production, and created a need for imported food. The growing dependence on imported food has removed the possibility of utilizing trade, specifically imports, for economic growth and development. Food imports merely maintain the status quo. At the same time these policies have forced government to pay out of its own revenues subsidies for the maintenance of lower food prices than exist on the world markets.

The continuation of policies of subsidizing food prices has exacerbated the trend of movement of people from rural areas to urban areas. Thus, an additional reason for encouraging realistic producer prices is to help forestall the continuing flood of people into unprepared cities.

Part of the problem results from the nature of many African governments today. Many African government officials would seem to view their role not as public officials but as private actors carrying the public mantle. Their efforts are frequently for their own private benefit or for the benefit of friends or relatives—what outsiders (and many insiders) view as corruption. Thus, an important factor to consider in trying to address the economic growth needs of Africa is the need to make more public the actions of government officials.

Another important factor to watch is the percent of GNP taken up by the government. In a recent study, the IMF identified Africa as having the highest percent of GNP taken up by government budgets and other government efforts. Such a situation crowds out private efforts in both credit availability and opportunity, reflects harmful tax and tariff policies, and generally means slow growth. The facts are striking—in 1978, in the United States, only 4.4 percent of the capital being formed came from publicly owned enterprises; in Germany, the figure was 10.8 percent; and in Japan, 11.2 percent. In comparison, in Algeria it was 67.6 percent, and in Zambia, 61.2 percent. The continent average was 32.4 percent. Government spending levels must be reduced, at least to where their growth is below the growth of GNP.

Overvalued currencies often discourage exports and encourage imports, reducing the attractiveness of foreign and indigenous investment in export industries. A realistic exchange rate is a very important factor.

A little earlier I indicated that several mechanisms for freeing up the marketplace were on the agenda of this conference. Let me mention eight needs here which I believe to be of particular importance:

1. The need to understand the unique contribution of the entrepreneur. Such a person should be encouraged and given the skills that would supplement natural inclinations. Such people are different from public sector functionaries and corporate bureaucrats. They are the sparks that can ignite the economy. They personally assume risk, manage, and produce goods or provide services themselves. Little is known about successful African entrepreneurs.

2. The need to realize the key role of small and medium-sized businesses as vehicles of growth.

3. The need to stimulate financial intermediaries. The goals here should be to broaden and deepen equity participation within the economy.

4. The need to resolve problems of capital availability. This means stimulating venture capital, devising mutual fund possibilities, utilizing development banks, and finding privately owned lending facilities to encourage private enterprise, and other mechanisms.

5. The need to devise tax and other incentives for entrepreneurial development.

6. The need to realize that services industries play a major role in modern economies and to encourage the development of services industries in Africa.

7. The need to identify those sectors of the economy where a private sector is most likely to develop and for governments to withdraw from those sectors. Such areas as transport, artisanry, and small-scale manufacturing are among several that come immediately to mind. Many countries have a vibrant informal, or underground, economy. With appropriate policies, these activities can be brought into the mainstream and not lose their dynamism.

8. The need to devise a way to make ethnicity an economic asset, not an economic liability.

A special mention must be made of the issue of private investment, particularly foreign private investment. You all know that I come from a country that prides itself in its faith in private investment. It is also a country whose citizens have a strong streak of nationalism and pride. The citizens of most countries feel a similar nationalism and pride. Yet, in the case of the United States, we have seen in recent years not the erection of new barriers to foreign investment but new efforts to attract it. States vie with each other by sending investment missions to foreign countries. State legislatures change laws to provide incentives for foreigners. The result has been that, during the 1980s, the United States has been world's largest recipient of foreign investment. We are pleased when foreigners contribute to our growth.

How does this compare with Africa? In most of Africa, foreign investment has often been viewed as an affront by nationalists. There has been a fear of losing control of the economy to foreigners. In order to bring technology and retain control, turn-key projects have been popular, and government-owned parastatals have been even more popular. Many of these investments, however, have been uneconomic. They remain as white elephants, inactive, or as a continuing burden to the government's budget and to the economy.

The market is the best test of investment needs. Private investment ensures an efficient and economic use of resources. Attitude is an important factor. Foreign investment is fungible—it will go where it is wanted and where opportunity exists. Look at the money in foreign bank accounts, in foreign real estate, or just plain hidden away. An additional factor for several countries is the heavy dependence on foreign workers who, while performing valuable technical services, still repatriate their savings, thus denying the host countries of a needed source of investment capital.

Earlier this year, the World Bank projected a disastrous decline in the flow of capital to Africa. Unless additional capital is found, the net flow will decline from $11 billion in 1980–1982 to $5 billion in 1985–1987. That problem must be addressed by African leaders, foreign countries, public and private sectors, and multilateral institutions.

A good portion of the debt crisis in which many African countries find themselves today results from a lack of confidence in—indeed a suspicion of—foreign investment. Faced with the obvious fact that capital was necessary for growth and expansion, many countries pursued domestic policies that discouraged investment by their own citizens and, for many reasons, were unwilling to accept foreign investment. The only available alternative was bank loans. Many of these loans went for nonproductive purposes and now have to be paid back without additional growth to produce new revenue. With the control of inflation, especially in the United States, the face value of these loans has proved to be even more onerous than might have been true during the 1970s. A desire to avoid future debt problems and to repay current debt is therefore an additional argument for encouraging investment.

How will these matters be brought to public attention? Unfortunately, few businessmen and businesswomen in Africa have a public policy agenda for consideration by government leaders. The business community is often demoralized, struggling with an inferiority complex that has derived from a public failure to appreciate how necessary to growth the business class is and from years of intellectual criticism of that class. Youth have stayed out of business because its image is bad. Many foreign advisers to African governments and professors in universities were, indeed still are, either skeptical or critical of the market. They favored control, rather than dynamism. The results have proved them wrong. As has happened in China, this distortion and discrediting need to be replaced by an alternative approach that places faith in the marketplace.

If you want your country to be among the developed countries of the world a century from now, what is needed? Economic growth alone will take it there. But you cannot have growth and the employment associated with it if, at the same time, you hate the job creators.

I could not make this presentation without a few words about the type of organization with which I now work—business organizations. They may be chambers of commerce, or they may have other names. In some places, they may not exist at all. What I am referring to is the need for institutions that will

- raise the level of public understanding of economic policy, of the choices and effects of various actions;
- be organized to reflect and encourage local, not national, interests, growth, and welfare;
- show government where rules and regulations stifle initiative and opportunity;
- present a positive image of business and combat from within corruption and corrupting monopolistic practices;
- be a source for training and new ideas;
- assist efforts and policies aimed at promoting economic diversification; and,
- institutionalize business presence.

Conclusion

Sustained rapid economic growth does not occur by accident. It is the logical result of a coherent set of policies designed to unleash the creative spirit and enterprise of the people. Few, if any, African countries have yet figured out what those policies are. The number one challenge to the public sector is to devise policies that will free up the private sector. Policies and people, not resources, are the prime determinants of growth. I am optimistic that this conference will be a major step in helping those who are interested in finding ways to enable African economic growth. Let me emphasize what I said earlier—the problems are solvable.

7

Private Initiative in Africa: A Problem of Clarity

Iba der Thiam

Minister of National Education,
Republic of Senegal

Reflection on the role that private initiative can or must play in the development of our African countries calls for an analytic distinction between the private and the public sectors of the economy. Beyond this, it calls for reflection on the differences between social alternatives.

Theoretical economic models often contradict each other. Some put great confidence in private initiative, arguing that from the free play of particular interests a better social order will emerge in which all gain. Diametrically opposed models limit the confidence they put in the individual, granting the public sector alone the ability to organize production and exchange in the best manner.

One can analyze these models by themselves, testing their internal coherence and gauging their potential effectiveness. But one thing is certain: No actual society is the perfect realization of pure theory. One country, known for its espousal of free enterprise, does not hesitate to intervene in important economic sectors, whether to effect specific or structural changes. Another country, ostensibly a strong defender of state planning, may allow a significant share of its economic activity to pass in a private sector that it tolerates but does not encourage.

Africa is no exception to the rule that the most marked theoretical oppositions lose their force when they come into contact with reality, which is always more intricate than the discussions we hold about it. This rule, however, manifests itself only in certain circumstances. For this reason, I would like to begin by noting cultural and historical reasons particular to our continent that make any conception opposing private initiative and state action a largely illusory construction.

Colonization has deeply changed the structures of our traditional societies, and the association of our economy with the world market has brought in its turn fresh perturbations. But every change leans against what it transforms, and there is no change, however deep, that does not preserve something of what it is changing. I am therefore convinced there exists an African type of economy, a type deeply rooted in our past, which is still present according to its own modalities. It would be a mistake to cover these modalities over with ideas and forms that are effective elsewhere but quickly show themselves to be impracticable here in Africa.

What are the most characteristic features of precolonial African societies? Even though information on this period of our past is for the moment negligible, the works left by Arab historians and Portuguese travellers (even though of relatively late date) make it possible for us to determine the principal human activities. African civilizations of this epoch were mostly agrarian. They were based, in the words of Balandier, "on age, sex, family structure, and a network of alliances."

The African economy was rooted in subsistence agriculture and in general was labor intensive and technologically simple. Very seldom could it produce large surpluses. It was an economy based as well on hunting, fishing, and picking fruits. To these activities we may add in certain cases mining, local artisanry, and some trading activities that took place in regularly convened markets despite a lack of good means of communication and transport within the village, the region, and more seldom, the kingdom.

In this context, modes of production were usually family based, rarely giving rise to antagonism and conflict strong enough to determine social classes in the Marxist sense. This does not mean that there were no social or economic contradictions or that conflicts of interest were totally absent. But traditional societies did have at their disposal all manner of integrating mechanisms. Even in societies in which every citizen, by virtue of his or her rank in the social structure, might harbor feelings of superiority or inferiority, his or her self-awareness was not defined in terms of exploitation, alienation, or domination— in short, in terms of class struggle.

The social antagonisms, both individual and clanic, that existed in these societies did not assume the divisive nature they assumed else- where—for at least four reasons. First, a whole ideological development founded, justified, diminished, and even covered over inequality in social or economic conditions and hierarchical relations. Second, deeply held norms regarding property and access to power, and hence political and economic preeminence, tempered the transitory frustrations that some people could feel. Third, land, at the time the principal means of production, was held collectively, a mechanism preventing private appropriation. Finally, African notions of goods and services were understood and dealt with in a particularly original and different manner.

In the developed societies of the West, where economic structures are usually more numerous and independent, property appears to be depersonalized—that is, without relation to specific individuals. When property is desired for its own meaning and value, it draws from this status an objective, measurable, universal unit—namely, money. From that moment, the personalities, the economic positions, the social or hierarchical positions of the individuals involved in the exchange fade away completely. What becomes important is the value of the elements exchanged. The depersonalization of property following the introduction of money is accompanied by a depersonalization of social relations and a humanization of relations between individuals.

Thus in modern industrial societies, the value of every property is measured and defined before all else by its production cost. The latter is fixed not by a person who might be influenced but by the obscure and inhuman play of inexorable economic laws.

On the contrary, in precolonial black Africa among communal agricultural societies that were barely monetized, property does not appear to have had the same objective meaning. It was valued and exchanged less according to abstract economic laws than through a network of interpersonal social relationships; in terms of the identity and status of the partners involved; according to the norms of prestige and assistance; in the framework of an ethic based on the principle of the gift and countergift.

Thus any property belonging to a traditional Wolof belonged and today still belongs to God, to the whole family, and to all the neighbors. To use it, the Wolof ran the risk (and today still runs the risk) of evoking harsh and pernicious criticism.

One of the most important and direct consequences of this belief system was that feasts, baptisms, marriages, funerals, and circumcisions had to serve for social regulation. These ceremonies provided opportunities to redistribute and circulate goods and riches. Therefore, they constituted a mechanism of economic equilibrium, of social and political harmony, which, according to a larger code of obligations, was based either on the duty of lavishness imposed on the most fortunate people or on rules for solidarity, cooperation, and assistance to the advantage of the dispossessed. This social mechanism aimed at reducing inequalities, at sharing among all in order to reinforce social cohesion, and at ensuring the integration of all groups within the community.

We can see, then, how the notion of property of precolonial African societies may be different from that which prevails in modern European societies. An even greater difference is observed in the case of African and Western notions about labor and services.

In modern societies based on industry and wage labor, labor is negotiated as an economic good. As such, it is submitted to market laws wherein the relations between supply and demand determine its price. In precolonial black African societies, on the contrary, labor appears to have had less of an autonomous role, less of a force independent of the individual. Rather, labor was a community activity logically emerging from norms of social life imposed by social convention.

Hence a hierarchy of professions is set up by the social opinion; hence labor depends on the individual's social status: "[Labor's] acquisition and its transfer are entirely governed by the system of social relations; its alienation is unthinkable. [Wage labor] would constitute a social apostasy. Since work cannot be sold, its provision calls for no specific remuneration. Moreover it always takes on a cooperative form."[1]

Under these conditions, the usage of labor did not necessarily entail a salary—a remuneration equivalent to the effort given, to the time spent, to the skills supplied—but simply to the obligations of the gift: food, assistance, sometimes care, all left to the discretion of the beneficiary. For example, the Peul expression *Wujungel ngese,* literally translated as "to steal a field," designates the practice of cultivating a plot of land that belongs to a relative—an uncle, a brother, or a cousin—without letting the relative know beforehand. The relative then determines the reward for the voluntary workers, giving them a bull, offering them a banquet, or giving them money. The gift by the beneficiary of Wujungel was always substantial and was more highly valued than the work done.

According to the principles of collective morality, the beneficiary was always bound to reward the act and its symbolism much more than to repay the precise commercial value of the given services. In fact, as noted by M. Cheikh Anta Diop: "Generosity was considered as an essential moral value; so much so that tradition reports that a lag [a knight] could not 'crack' a kola nut alone without losing his honor; [if] in solitude, when there is nobody to share it with, he must throw away the other piece."

Similarly, the *nadtirgol,* a term used by the Peuls (called *naadante* by the Wolofs) denotes an almost cooperative system of labor on all the village fields, following a principle of rotation determined by a common agreement and observed by all.

Such is the substratum of African economic practice, a substratum that we must refrain from regarding as only residual today and appearing only in the form of survivals more or less doomed to disappearance. Perhaps because Africa has never known a technological revolution, the continent has not undergone the process of accumulation of capital that leads to the creation of economic feudalities. In other societies, by the characteristic logic of profit, such feudalities end up appearing as a sort of cyst in the society; they channel all behavior toward the advancement of their particular interests. In our societies, on the contrary, the possession of any property, and, a fortiori, of great wealth, entails a whole series of obligations. Therefore, the distinction between private and public in African societies is not as clear cut as it is elsewhere.

So it seems clear to me that the theory according to which private initiative and state action must be opposed to each other loses much of its pertinence in this environment. The real debate lies elsewhere. Instead of binding ourselves to a paradigm that does violence to the African reality, we must proclaim the fundamental complementarity of the private and public sectors; and it is by this complementarity that Africa can achieve self-sustaining development. Africa must benefit from both private and public investments at the same time. Desire for profit makes private initiative anxious about good management and productivity. The spirit of enterprise, risk-bearing ability, and boldness in innovation—these three qualities associated with private initiative in economic matters can only be beneficial to our countries whether in the industrial and commercial fields or in that of services. In particular, the development of small and medium-scale enterprises is most desirable.

Public investments go to enterprises of public interest which, because of their strategic nature with regard to development, as well as because of the great amounts of capital they inject into the development process, suggest that public authority should play a role of management and supervision. A well-managed state enterprise is just as capable of creating productive employment and contributing powerfully to development as the private sector; sluggish bureaucracy and the icy convolutions of management without imagination do not necessarily constitute an overriding danger for public enterprise.

Development policy, enterprise creation, and technology transfer depend on the mobilization of capital. But the volume of savings is generally insufficient in our countries, and for whatever reasons this lack of capital will only put a brake on development.

The first solution consists in welcoming foreign capital, public as well as private. The management of both is carried out according to standardized norms in different sectors, but despite this, it is hard to imagine how Africa can, at the present stage of its development, refuse to appeal for foreign investment. If groups, whether national or international, propose investments that will result in the creation of jobs, social and economic advancement, and a greater welfare for the people concerned there are no reasons whatever to refuse these requests (except pure sectarianism). It is necessary, however, to make sure that the introduction of private capital, especially in the form of multinational corporations, does not translate into a surrender of national sovereignty, that it does not prejudice our cultural identity, that it does not increase social inequalities, or that it does not encourage the emergence of rival economic powers, capable of discrediting the government in the minds of the public. Thus the needed opening of our economies to outside capital must go hand in hand with a strict sense of respect for balance and a precise definition of the rights and duties of each party.

However, it is not a question of placing all our expectations on outside initiatives. They have their objective limits, and even if the precautions I have just enumerated are taken, we cannot be satisfied with a situation in which risks of dependency can take alarming proportions. It is therefore imperative for us to work on the strengthening of national savings and investment. The state budget must be capable not only of financing the running of public services; it must also contribute to productive investments, giving these much greater importance than it does at present.

The problem of national savings in Africa is particularly acute; the direction our development will follow depends most of all on our capacity to solve it. As we are able or unable to mobilize higher levels of saving and to organize novelly and systematically the efforts that the populations are ready to devote to economic development, the prospect of well-being we hope for will be opened or shut.

This is all the more urgent because the 1980s are, for Africa, a decade of multiple challenges. If the world economy looks grim, the estimates for African economies are far more alarming. The harmful effects of malnutrition and famine are felt everywhere, worsened by a persistent drought that makes food provision more problematic each year. The indicators for education and health are very poor. Efforts to eradicate illiteracy and establish an acceptable medical framework have far to go. A massive rural exodus uproots peasants in quest of hypothetical city jobs. Juvenile delinquency is increasing, and even university graduates are hit by unemployment.

And besides, the international environment is far from favorable. The deterioration of Africa's terms of trade has not stopped. The continuous rise of the dollar that the U.S. policy of high interest rates fails to arrest (indeed, quite the contrary) weighs heavily against the capacity of our countries to pay back our large debts. The Western countries, themselves suffering the effects of a persisting economic crisis, are inclined to diminish the share of their resources devoted to development aid. We could easily lengthen this list of dangers to our economies and the destabilizing risks they entail.

For these many challenges, we must mobilize all our energies in appealing to private initiative together with state action. This process must take into account the African particularities I have discussed. By freeing ourselves from schemes poorly adapted to African realities—schemes that express ideological and narrowly dogmatic conceptions a priori—and turning to our own paradigm we can give ourselves a chance of success. It is not a question of requiring originality for originality's sake but simply of being realistic.

African development, if we want it to be genuine—different from the mirages that accompany artificial and copied solutions—must be endogenous. Endogenous development presupposes that the steps adopted by each nation may differ, as the same solutions do not always apply everywhere. Each nation must find its own path, appropriate to its regime type, national economic structure, and the particular challenges it faces.

Notes

1. Bezy Fernand, *L'Organisation Economique des Societes Traditionelles,* in *Dossier Afrique,* Marabout Universite, no. 220, 1971, p. 217.

8

Foreign Debts and African Economies with Special Reference to West Africa

Roland E. Ubogu
University of Lagos

The problem of foreign debt of many developing countries has been a major subject of international debate for a number of years. A new facet, and one that is disquieting when looked at against the background of the damped prospects of development of world trade, is the direction and pace of new indebtedness and terms for some developing countries. The debt position of many West African countries is far more precarious than the picture reflected in the problems of the few developing countries that have attracted widespread attention as the largest debtors.

The debt service ratios for most developing countries and, particularly those of Africa, have worsened dramatically since 1970. The number of rescheduling operations in these countries has rocketed, as shown in Table 8.1. Table 8.1 shows that many developing countries have since 1975 faced the problem of debt payment as initially scheduled. The burden has been on the increase as reflected by the rise in volume of debt from $478 million in 1975 to $40 billion in 1982.

As a result of the problems of debt repayment, many African countries have pursued policies detrimental to their long-term development interests, such as a retrenchment policy of decreasing imports to improve their external financial positions. Others that have not been able to reduce imports have resorted to debt rescheduling under the auspices of the Paris Club. The African countries' reschedulings are shown in Table 8.2. Of the seventeen countries listed in Table 8.2, seven are in West Africa. As the number of African countries seeking and actually rescheduling their foreign debts increased, the amount of rescheduled debt also increased from $550 million in 1980 to $5 billion in 1983.

Table 8.1 Multilateral Rescheduling Operation of Debts Towards Official
Private Creditors

Year	Number of Cases	Volume in U.S.$ million
1975	2	478
1976	2	480
1977	3	382
1978	2	2,312
1979	4	4,920
1980	6	4,459
1981	14	10,786
1982	22	40,000

Source: H. Wilkens, "The Debt Burden of Developing Countries," Economica 28
(1983):40.

This radical rise in debt burden of African countries has serious
implications not only for the internal development of these countries
but also for the operational capacity of the international financial
system. Whereas for the economies of African countries, the overall
burden of all external liabilities is decisive, for the world financial
system, primarily the relations between the banks and the African
nations are important. Even a relatively small volume of debt can
pose great problems for the economy of small countries like those of

Table 8.2 Rescheduling of External Debts in Africa 1966-1983

Country	Years of Rescheduling				Number of Times
Central African Republic		1981	1983		2
Egypt		1976			1
Ghana	1966	1968	1970	1974	4
Gabon		1978			1
Liberia	1977	1980	1981	1982	4
Madagascar	1981	1982	1983		3
Malawi		1982	1983		2
Morocco		1983			1
Mauritania		1981	1982		2
Nigeria		1983			1
Senegal	1981	1982	1983		3
Sierra Leone	1977	1980	1982		3
Sudan	1979	1980	1981	1982	4
Togo	1979	1980	1981	1982	4
Uganda		1981	1982		2
Zaire	1976	1977	1979	1980	
		1981	1982		6
Zambia		1983			1

Source: A. Adedeji, "Foreign Debt and the Prospects of Growth in the
Developing Countries of Africa in the 1980's," paper presented at Conference
on Foreign Debt and Nigeria's Economic Development in Lagos, March 5-6, 1984,
p. 3.

Table 8.3 Debts of Highly Indebted African Countries in 1980

Country	Amount Outstanding ($ million)	Debts/GNP Ratio (%)	Debts per Capita ($)
Mauritania	750	143	460
Congo	1,150	104	760
Togo	950	93	380
Gambia	150	86	210
Somalia	750	85	190
Morocco	7,800	78	390
Guinea	1,200	74	220
Zambia	2,300	71	400
Zaire	4,350	69	150
Egypt	15,050	65	380
Gabon	1,500	62	2,270
Malawi	800	58	140

Source: H. Wilkens, "The Debt Burden of Developing Countries," Economica 28 (1983):41.

West Africa. This fact is often ignored in the current external debt debate.

As Table 8.3 indicates, the smallest countries bear the largest debt in relation to the GNP. Although the problem of external indebtedness of African countries is not an entirely new phenomenon, the issues involved in the current problems faced by these countries are just now being adequately articulated. There is still a lack of sufficient knowledge on the nature of the problems.

The literature on external debt problems views the debt issue as a process characterized by a relationship between debt and export earnings. It is believed that the external debt of these countries is caused by an increasing gap between domestic savings and investment and export earnings. As the gap widens and debt accumulates, interest charges also build up and a country must therefore borrow increasing amounts solely to maintain a constant flow of imports. To escape this trap, national income must grow at a reasonable rate because the capacity to service debt depends mainly on the continuing growth of output. Otherwise it will not be possible to close the gap between domestic savings and investment.

This chapter examines the main issues of the external indebtedness of West African countries in particular and of Africa in general with a view to identifying the nature and causes of the problem. After this examination, some possible solutions will be prescribed. The chapter is divided into four sections. Section I examines the structure of the West African/African countries external debt, whereas Section II is concerned with analyzing the possible causes of these countries' external indebtedness. In Section III, I examine the problems of debt management in these countries and propose some possible solutions. Section IV concludes the chapter with policy recommendations.

Section I: The Structure of the West African Countries' External Debt

Although complete statistical data covering all of the West African countries do not exist, the information in Tables 8.4 and 8.5 shows that total outstanding debt of West African nations increased from $2.5 billion in 1967 to $3.2 billion in 1970 and by 1977 it had risen to $11.9 billion. This represented an overall increase of 376 percent for the ten-year period. Total disbursed debt on the other hand increased slowly from $2.0 billion in 1967 to $2.1 billion in 1970 and thereafter rose rapidly to $7.1 billion in 1977. The combined outstanding and disbursed debt for the region increased from $4.5 billion in 1967 to $19.0 billion in 1977, representing overall a phenomenal increase of 322 percent within the decade.

The annual average growth rate of total external debt was about 42 percent, which is much higher than the average growth rate of gross domestic product (GDP) and export of goods and services. It can be argued that debt service matters more than total outstanding and disbursed debts. An examination of Tables 8.4 and 8.5 indicates that total debt service for the West African subregion rose from $128.4 million in 1967 to $716.2 million in 1977, representing an overall increase of 558 percent for the period. The average annual rate of growth of debt service is about 50 percent, significantly higher than that of GDP and exports. Consequently West African economies cannot on the basis of the growth of their income and exports meet their annual debt service obligations. This explains why some of these countries have resorted to rescheduling of their debts over a much longer period of payment.

A critical examination of the structure of West African countries' external debts in terms of the share of outstanding, disbursed, and debt service in GDP and exports shows that only in two countries (Niger and Burkina Faso) was the ratio of outstanding debt to GDP less than 10 percent in 1967. The ratio ranged from 7.1 percent for Burkina Faso (formerly Upper Volta) to as high as 127.6 percent for Mali (see Table 8.6). On the other hand, for no country in 1970 was the outstanding debt/GDP ratio less than 10 percent.

In 1976, the ratios ranged from 10.2 percent for Niger to 113.3 percent for Mali. The situation became more precarious in 1977 when this ratio was not below 17.3 percent except for Nigeria, an oil-exporting

Table 8.4 External Debt Outstanding, Disbursed, Service, GDP, and Exports of West African Countries (US$ million)

COUNTRY	1967 Debt Out- standing	1967 Debt Dis- bursed	1967 Debt Service	1967 GDP	1967 Exports	1970 Debt Out- standing	1970 Debt Dis- bursed	1970 Debt Service	1970 GDP	1970 Exports
Benin	43	39.6	1.0	215.1	36.0	49.3	34.0	2.1	238.4	74.2
Cameroon	96.4	53.2	2.1	787.8	202.8	234.6	130.8	9.0	1008.3	289.6
Central African Republic	18.5	18.1	1.5	178.6	53.3	30.2	19.9	1.9	197.7	62.2
Chad	37.5	25.5	2.5	234.1	55.0	43.3	33.9	2.3	241.6	72.5
Gambia	-	-	-	-	-	10.6	5.1	0.1	36.7	19.3
Ghana	527.6	526.6	22.4	1535	311.4	557.6	487.2	23.6	2304.7	472.4
Guinea	209.6	222.3	4.7	376.7	50.9	268.3	10.4	11.5	413.1	50.8
Ivory Coast	252.2	165.3	28.8	1111.4	640.7	423.4	255.4	38.6	1490.8	439.9
Liberia	173.2	155.5	9.8	300.7	161.9	175.4	156.1	17.3	374.0	216.9
Mali	286.5	188.2	4.5	224.5	41.4	287.9	236.2	0.9	254.2	66.6
Mauritania	31.6	20.5	1.1	160.4	81.5	40.3	27.1	3.2	172.5	105.2
Niger	31.4	14.5	1.3	395.3	55.3	86.3	35.8	2.1	366.2	56.6
Nigeria	598.0	382.4	36.2	1966.	729.1	690.7	458.9	54.	3514.3	1335
Senegal	89.8	62.1	3.8	740	199.7	142.0	102	5.4	733.9	247.3
Sierra Leone	70.5	65.6	6.8	188.4	83.5	89.6	66.0	11.0	278.8	119.4
Togo	35.9	31.1	1.4	213.4	57.2	43.7	36.6	2.4	240.2	78.0
Burkina Faso	20.9	16.2	0.5	294.5	27.4	32.4	20.5	1.9	317.6	32.1
TOTAL	2522.5	1987.7	128.4	8921.9	2787.1	3205.6	2115.9	187.3	12183	3738

Source: World Tables, 1976 and 1980 (Baltimore: John Hopkins University Press, 1976 and 1980).

country. The data in Table 8.8 clearly show the increasing debt burden of the region with the ratio increasing up to 152.6 percent for Mauritania in 1977. The picture is no more sanguine when one considers the disbursed debt/GDP ratio for each of the countries. The data in Tables 8.6, 8.7, and 8.8 demonstrate that there was a significant upward trend in this ratio between 1967 and 1977.

In 1967 the disbursed debt/GDP ratio ranged from 3.7 percent for Niger to 83.8 percent for Mali (Table 8.6). In 1977 there was no country with a ratio below 13.4 percent except Nigeria. In fact the ratio varied between 13.4 percent for Niger to as high as 64.5 percent for Mali. As regards the ratio of outstanding and disbursed debt to

Table 8.5 External Debt Outstanding, Disbursed, Service, and Share of Interest Payment for West African Countries (US$ million)

COUNTRY	Debt Out-standing	Debt Disbursed	Debt Service	GDP	Exports	Interest Share in Debt Service ('70)	Int. share in Debt Svc ('77)
Benin	237.3	133.8	9.7	603.2	159.2	38.1	23.7
Cameroon	1208.1	749.3	65.9	2712	1030.5	51.1	46.1
Central African Republic	147.1	115.4	6.2	435.1	135.0	15.8	22.6
Chad	244.7	116.5	13.1	532.4	139.4	13.0	19.1
Gambia	86.3	23.4	0.3	112.4	65.8	-	-
Ghana	1050.1	785.0	37.2	14327.8	1017.8	49.6	43.0
Guinea	-	-	-	-	-	-	-
Ivory Coast	3640.2	1973.2	290.2	6441.6	2731.9	30.3	35.7
Liberia	387.2	265.8	23.4	861.2	470.2	34.7	35.0
Mali	683.3	448.9	6.6	696.3	148.5	33.3	36.4
Mauritania	677.9	457.4	41.1	444.1	178.9	9.4	22.1
Niger	267.1	122.2	9.5	911.8	178.3	33.3	33.7
Senegal	812.3	440.6	58.6	1931.0	687.9	24.1	35.8
Sierra Leone	249.9	190.2	16.6	643.4	167.1	22.7	28.9
Togo	575.9	284.5	25	668.8	215.7	37.5	26
Burkina Faso	293.7	134.9	6.2	683.8	104.6	15.8	30.6
TOTAL	11899.9	7132.5	716.2	72153	20351.7	-	-

Source: World Tables, 1976 and 1980 (Baltimore: John Hopkins University Press, 1976 and 1980).

GDP, it was between 32.8 percent for Ghana and 255.6 percent for Mauritania in 1967, compared to its variation between 11.6 percent for Niger and 255.6 percent for Mauritania, the highest debtor in 1977.

Many West African countries take loans from the international financial market to develop their economies by increasing their export of goods and services. It is therefore expected that an increasingly favorable ratio of exports to imports should allow a government to pay for such loans and their interest on annual basis. Consequently it is necessary to examine the share of outstanding, disbursed, and debt service in exports for the various countries. The data in Tables 8.6 and 8.8 indicate that no country had the ratio of outstanding debt to export less than 34.7 percent in 1967. There were five countries— Cameroon, Central African Republic, Ivory Coast, Mauritania, and

Table 8.6 Share of Debt Outstanding, Disbursed, and Debt Service in GDP and Exports for West African Countries (%), 1967

COUNTRY	Debt Out-standing in GDP	Disbursed Debt in GDP	Debt Service in GDP	Debt Out-standing in Exports	Disbursed Debt in Exports	Debt Service in Exports
Benin	20	18.4	0.5	119.4	110	2.8
Cameroon	12.2	6.8	0.3	47.5	26.2	1.0
Central African Republic	10.4	10.1	0.8	34.7	34	2.8
Chad	16.0	11.3	1.1	68.2	48.2	4.5
Gambia	-	-	-	-	-	-
Ghana	34.4	34.3	1.5	169.4	169.1	7.2
Guinea	55.6	53.7	1.2	411.8	436.7	9.2
Ivory Coast	22.7	14.9	2.6	39.4	25.8	4.5
Liberia	57.6	51.7	3.3	107	90	6.1
Mali	127.6	83.8	2.0	692	454.6	10.9
Mauritania	19.7	12.8	0.7	38.8	25.2	1.3
Niger	7.9	3.7	0.3	56.8	26.2	2.4
Nigeria	30.4	19.5	1.8	82	52.4	5.0
Senegal	12.1	8.4	0.5	45	31.1	1.9
Sierra Leone	37.4	34.8	3.6	84.4	78.6	8.1
Togo	16.8	14.6	0.7	62.8	54.4	2.4
Burkina Faso	7.1	5.5	0.2	76.3	59.1	1.8

Source: Calculated by the author from Table 8.4.

Senegal—with their ratio less than 50 percent but greater than 34.7 percent, whereas six countries' ratio varied between 56.8 and 84.4 percent. The remaining countries—Mali, Liberia, Guinea, Ghana and Benin—had ratios exceeding 100 percent. Of these sixteen countries, ten had outstanding debt/export ratios ranging from 103.2 percent to 175.5 percent whereas four others had ratios above 200 percent (Burkina Faso, 280.8 percent; Togo, 267 percent; Mauritania, 378.9 percent; Mali, 460.1 percent).

The share of disbursed debt in exports varied among the West African countries from 26.2 percent for Cameroon to 454.6 percent

Table 8.7 Share of Debt Outstanding, Disbursed, and Debt Service in GDP and Exports for
West African Countries (%) 1970

COUNTRY	Debt Out-standing in GDP	Disbursed Debt in GDP	Debt Service in GDP	Debt Out-standing in Exports	Disbursed Debt in Exports	Debt Service in Exports
Benin	20.7	14.3	0.9	66.4	45.8	2.8
Cameroon	23.3	13	0.9	81	45.2	3.1
Central African Republic	15.3	10.1	1.0	48.6	32	3.1
Chad	17.9	14	1.0	59.7	46.8	3.2
Gambia	28.9	13.9	0.3	54.9	26.4	0.5
Ghana	24.2	21.1	0.1	118	103.1	5.0
Guinea	64.9	2.5	2.8	528.1	20.5	22.6
Ivory Coast	28.4	17.1	2.6	96.2	58.1	8.8
Liberia	46.9	41.7	4.6	80.9	72	8.0
Mali	113.3	92.9	0.4	432.3	354.7	1.4
Mauritania	23.4	15.7	1.9	38.3	25.8	3.0
Niger	23.6	9.8	0.6	152.5	63.3	3.7
Nigeria	19.7	13.1	1.5	51.7	34.4	4.0
Senegal	19.3	13.9	0.7	57.4	41.2	2.1
Sierra Leone	32.1	23.7	4.0	75	55.3	9.2
Togo	18.2	15.2	1.0	56	46.9	3.1
Burkina Faso	10.2	6.5	0.6	100.9	63.9	5.9

Source: Calculated by the author from Table 8.4.

for Mali in 1967. Although in 1977 it went from 35.6 percent for Gambia to 302.2 percent for Mali, the only exception was Nigeria with a ratio of 6.9 percent. The degree of indebtedness is more pronounced when the ratio of combined outstanding and disbursed debt in exports is calculated.

One argument often posed in the literature is that what matters to a nation is its debt service and not necessarily outstanding or disbursed debts. As long as a country's net export receipts are sufficient to meet

Table 8.8 Share of Debt Outstanding, Disbursed, and Debt Service in GDP and Exports for West
African Countries (%), 1977

COUNTRY	Debt Out-standing in GDP	Disbursed Debt in GDP	Debt Service in GDP	Debt Out-standing in Exports	Disbursed Debt in Exports	Debt Service in Exports
Benin	39.3	22.2	1.6	149.1	84	6.1
Cameroon	44.5	27.6	2.4	117.2	72.7	6.4
Central African Republic	33.8	26.5	1.4	109	85.5	4.6
Chad	46	21.9	2.5	175.5	83.6	9.4
Gambia	76.8	20.8	0.3	131.1	35.6	0.5
Ghana	17.3	15.5	0.3	103.2	77.1	3.7
Guinea	-	-	-	-	-	-
Ivory Coast	56.5	30.6	4.5	133.2	72.2	10.6
Liberia	45	30.9	2.7	82.3	56.5	5.0
Mali	98.1	64.5	0.9	460.1	302.2	4.4
Mauritania	152.6	103	9.3	378.9	255.7	23.0
Niger	29.3	13.4	1.0	149.8	68.5	5.3
Nigeria	3.3	2.2	0.3	10.4	6.9	0.8
Senegal	42.1	22.8	3.0	118.1	64.1	8.5
Sierra Leone	38.8	29.6	2.6	149.6	113.8	9.9
Togo	86.1	42.5	3.7	267	131.9	11.6
Burkina Faso	43	19.7	0.9	280.8	129.0	5.9

Source: Calculated by the author from Table 8.5.

its annual debt service obligations, the argument goes, the country is
credit worthy and can even borrow more. An analysis of the percentage
share of debt service in exports of the West African nations shows
that it ranged from 1 percent for Cameroon to 10.9 percent for Mali
among the countries in 1967. And, in 1977 it fluctuated from 0.5
percent for Gambia to 23 percent for Mauritania.

Although these percentages may appear to be relatively low, a look
at the rate of growth of their export earnings reveals either negative,

zero, or below 2 percent per annum declines. This implies that most of them are not even in a position to maintain their current import bills from export earnings. Consequently they will not be able to meet their debt obligations. This lack of growth in export earnings forced many of these countries to reschedule their loans. The increasing debt burden of the West African countries has not arisen solely from the payment of the loan principal but also from the interest payment. As a result of increases in the rate of interest on these loans caused by worldwide inflation, the share of interest on debt service over time has been increasing (see Table 8.5).

African Countries' Indebtedness

The problem of external indebtedness is not unique to West African countries but is characteristic of all developing nations. Total outstanding debt, for example, for all African countries was estimated for 1981 and 1982 at $81.8 and $96.2 billion, respectively.[1] The rate of increase of Africa's external indebtedness was found to be much greater than that for all other developing nations though it represented only 19 percent of total outstanding and disbursed debt in 1982. Another feature of Africa's debt problem is that its average annual debt growth rate of 23 percent was much greater than the rate of growth of African income and exports.

Furthermore there had been some structural changes in the composition of African debt. Within the 1970–1980 decade, the share of official creditors—both bilateral and multilateral—declined from 67.5 to 60.4 percent and that of private creditors increased from 32.5 to 39.5 percent. This structural change has had adverse effects on the African countries because they have had to pay higher interest and liquidate the loans within a shorter time as compared with official creditors.

Available data show that external outstanding and disbursed debt for Africa has been increasing continuously since 1970. But net capital inflows have been on the decline especially since 1978 after reaching a peak of $12 billion.[2] This decline in net financial inflows has resulted in adverse structural change in Africa's debt position. The reasons for the decline in public net financial inflows include increased amortization, which reduced total annual disbursements, and the reluctance since 1979 of private creditors to extend further credits to African nations. The other characteristics of the African debt are, therefore, privatization and deteriorating lending terms and conditions.

Privatization and Deteriorating
Lending Terms and Conditions

A special feature of the debt structure of African countries in general is the shift since 1970 from official to private sources of external finance. It has been estimated that private debts that were only 32.5 percent of total debt in 1971 have increased to 71.5 percent in 1980 and are expected to be 75 percent by the end of 1983. It was also estimated that loans from official sources that constituted 65 percent in 1972 had declined to 58 percent in 1982.[3]

Within official sources there were some structural changes as well. The share of multilateral sources declined from 81 to 67 percent and that of bilateral sources increased from 19 to 33 percent during the same period. The outcome of this structural shift in credit sources has been a decrease in the share of concessional loans and an increase in the share of loans contracted under variable high interest rates.

Apart from experiencing an increasing external debt incidence, African nations are also witnessing the tightening of terms of external borrowing. The overall cost of borrowing, for example, increased from 4 percent in 1972 to 10 percent in 1982 as a result of increases in interest rates in the private money markets, which skyrocketed from 7 to 14 percent during the 1970–1982 period. Furthermore, the average maturity of loans declined from 20 to 15 years with the grace period reduced from 6 to 4 years for most loans during the same period. Finally the grant elements of most official loans declined from 37 to 7 percent of total loans.

Section II: Possible Causes of External Indebtedness

The causes of West African countries indebtedness in particular and Africa in general can be traced to both internal and external factors that have formed a web of mutually reinforcing factors. The major causes are well articulated by A. Adedeji and H. Wilkens:

- A hard core of loans contracted after the first oil price increase, which, at that time, helped to overcome the crisis of adjustment easily and quickly.
- The further rise in the cost of energy imports as a result of the second oil price explosion.
- The worldwide recession and the consequent adverse trends in export volumes and prices especially for the raw materials that

are crucial for many African countries. Export earnings dropped against the background of escalating import bills.

- The sharp rise in the debt burden as a result of unfavorable borrowing conditions—in particular, high interest rates.
- The diminution of development aid from the advanced countries.
- Poor economic management followed by misuse of resources, corruption, and waste of public funds.
- The inadequate adjustment of most countries to changes in the world economic climate and especially to changes in price relationships.
- Bad debt management, that is, inability of countries to fully utilize external loans and aid to generate adequate surpluses for repayment of loans as well as service charges.
- Absence of adequate policies and institutions for domestic resource mobilization and management as an instrument for reducing external debt.
- Absence of fiscal and financial policy linkages with development resources.
- Negative role of transnational banks and financial institutions in resource flows to and out of Africa.
- Lack of coordination of aid donors policies at national level to ensure maximum economic impact of aid and loans packages on development.[4]

Overall, it seems that a major cause of Africa's indebtedness stems from deep-rooted structural economic problems. And associated with these problems are sectoral ones in the nature of debt servicing, lack of growth of export sales, worsening of terms of trade, inflation, high interest rates, and so on.

Continuous Decline in Export Earnings

The inability of many West African countries to meet debt service obligations is partly the result of a worldwide economic recession that has led to a decline in demand for primary commodity exports. The solution to Africa's debt problem therefore seems to lie in changing the basic structure of the countries' economies in relation to the international economic system. This means that the degree of difficulty in debt servicing depends mainly on the productive capacities and export performance of these countries. Only rapid export growth can, in the long run, ease the debt-servicing problems to a tolerable level.

Usually structural disequilibrium between import bills and export earnings forces many African countries to resort to borrowing. This means that a lack of sound import management policies is a common characteristic of African states. It seems to us that repayment of outstanding external debts requires a well-planned program of rapidly growing exports as a means of reducing current account deficits of these countries.

Restrictive Import Policy and Control

The debt service payments due on previously contracted external loans are creating serious problems of adjustment for many African countries in view of worldwide stagnation in demand, persistent high interest rates, and lack of new financial resources previously available. These nations cannot borrow their way out, and hence they have attempted to establish a new balance of payments equilibrium by pursuing restrictive import and budgetary policies.

The effects of this policy of adjustment are already being felt in some developing countries. Although restrictive import and budgetary policies have the advantage of reducing current account deficits, they have the adverse effect of reducing overall economic growth. What is required in African countries is very selective import restrictions on items that can be easily produced domestically such as food items and clothing, and not on essential raw materials and spare parts needed for industries. Second, there is an urgent need to reduce government expenditure on those social and economic services that can be fully paid for by the public, in addition to government wastage, corruption, overinflated contracts, and high subsidy on public utilities and services.

Fiscal and Financial Policies

The fiscal and monetary policy of a nation has a significant effect on its indebtedness. As a country's domestic economic situation worsens and the balance of payments position deteriorates, confidence in its economic management might weaken, leading to capital flight and a fall in net lending. Furthermore, with national output and exports declining, reserves almost exhausted, and debt-servicing obligations increasing, the nation's foreign exchange resources will continue to be inadequate to maintain existing levels of growth.

An issue associated with this situation is government policies on expenditure. In some instances West African countries in particular and Africa in general have borrowed from abroad to finance recurrent expenditures (on food imports, military and civil service payrolls, and delinquent projects). There has been borrowing for deficit financing. These are bad economic policies, and African nations must avoid them at all cost if they are to develop economically. There has been an enormous surge in borrowing during the last decade by African countries without consideration of the possibility of repayment and debt servicing.

Section III: Debt Management and Possible Solutions

Debt management is a new phenomenon in African economic policies since the problem of external debt has come to the fore during the last decade. Consequently, policymakers do not often realize that decisions regarding borrowing abroad have repercussions on a country's development objectives and priorities. The poor debt management policies of African nations contributed greatly to their present financial crisis.

The question is how debt management can best be incorporated in the development strategies of African countries to reduce the debt-servicing problem and allow progress toward economic development. To manage external debts effectively, it is important to project accurately the time profile of debt service obligations and forecast export earnings, domestic revenues, and future access to various sources to finance.

In an ideal situation, effective external debt management includes three specific interrelated processes: (1) defining the goal of the borrowing, (2) deciding how much and where to borrow, and (3) assessing the repayment capabilities. The core of external debt management therefore is the determination of how much foreign debt a country should contract over time and on what terms.

As part of external debt management, the methods of selecting the relevant available financing are very important. What is crucial is the choice of the best combination of external finance (loans, grants, or direct investment) suitable to the objectives of individual projects and the economy as a whole, which takes into account the profits, dividends, prepayments for exports, and cash flows. The cost of new debts must be analyzed in terms of maturity and interest attached to them with a view toward a tolerable debt structure.

A means of debt management that has become popular during the last twenty years is debt rescheduling. Most countries currently facing debt repayment problems have resorted to this form of financing (see Table 8.2). Although debt rescheduling offers temporary relief to a debt burden, the deep-rooted problems associated with it need to be considered carefully before a nation resorts to this policy alternative.

In addition to excessive borrowing, there is the basic problem of balance of payments whose origin lies in the nations' monetary and fiscal policies, inflation, overvalued exchange rates, stagnation of exports, and excessive growth of imports. Under such circumstances, a rescheduling of debt payments can only bring temporary relief, and unless the basic causes of the debt problem are tackled, it will merely postpone the problem. Therefore, a more lasting solution to the debt problems of West African countries in particular and Africa in general is to adopt appropriate economic development policies and productive investment plans that will encourage domestic production for consumption and export.

Rescheduling of debts should not be a common policy prescription to the African debt problems because it will cause creditors to require countries to adopt strict austerity measures that include devaluation and enforcement of credit controls, reduction in budgetary expenditures, and other deflationary measures. This may not necessarily be in the best interests of the debtor country. Hence, rescheduling should be a last resort solution to the external debt problem.

Section IV: Conclusion and Policy Prescriptions

This chapter has considered the structure of both West African and African countries' external debt. A tremendous increase in their total outstanding and disbursed debts, as well as in their debt service payments since 1967, has been observed. Many countries are now reneging on their debt obligations because of a lack of foreign exchange availability and resorting to rescheduling of debt payments. The possible causes of these countries external indebtedness were also examined, and it was found that they are related in both internal and external factors. Finally, the chapter has offered a brief analysis of the problems of debt management and provided some guidelines on how the West African countries might manage their external debts.

In conclusion, it was noted that African countries' external debt problems can best be solved by encouraging increased export earnings relative to import costs. Future prospects for economic growth depend on structural change within the economies themselves rather than on the international economic system. Africa faces enormous development and financial problems, but these are not insurmountable provided there is the political will and a clear-cut policy direction.

The recovery of the economies of the advanced nations that seems to be under way can only augur well for the development and growth prospects of Africa, if adequate and relevant domestic policies are adopted and implemented. The current African debt problems are enormous but manageable, provided that structural adjustment in production and trade takes place to meet the challenges posed.

Although the prospects for world growth appear impressive in the long run, these can only be achieved if both debtors and creditors in the international financial market realize the degree of their interdependence. No doubt the options and most relevant combinations of instruments for growth vary from country to country in Africa, but of paramount importance to all countries is the policy of careful borrowing to finance economic projects that can really generate the momentum for self-sustaining development.

The solution of the debt problem lies, therefore, in accepting the fact that African countries must restructure their monetary and financial policies both to meet the present emergencies and to generate additional growth. To achieve this, long-term financing based on concessionary terms, other than private commercial loans, should be contracted for the process of structural adjustment. The present rescheduling of debts should not be regarded as an end but as a means for long-term restructuring of the economies and development process, while the search for new avenues for domestic resource mobilization continues.

African countries also need to adopt drastic policy measures to reduce overspending, misuse, and waste of domestic resources. They must reduce their level of conspicuous consumption so that their external borrowing needs can be calculated more carefully so as to not exceed their probable net receipts. This approach is consistent with their own interests because the international machinery of finance and trade will impose drastic sanctions in the event of unilateral renunciation of debt service commitments.

There must also be drastic policy measures to discourage the present trend toward corruption and individual financial enrichment and excessive dependence on foreign technical and managerial consultancy services at exorbitant fees when nationals can perform such functions at much lower costs.

On the international level there should be close cooperation among the banks, the debtor, and creditor countries. The advanced nations should be prepared to provide adequate financing to the multilateral institutions such as the World Bank and the International Monetary Fund. This is necessary so that they can be in a better position to assist African countries. The IMF for its part should not prescribe the same solutions for all African countries in financial crisis so as to avoid triggering a spate of competitive devaluations by the countries concerned. The creditor banks and governments should be willing to provide a temporary cushion to African countries to cover temporary liquidity shortages.

Finally, to improve African countries' export earning capabilities and to be able to meet their debt-servicing obligations, industrial countries should open their markets wider to the products of these countries rather than closing them as has been practiced in the past. The advanced countries should also increase their official aids on favorable terms to African countries.

Notes

1. A. Adedeji, "Foreign Debt and the Prospects of Growth in the Developing Countries of Africa in the 1980's," paper presented at Conference on Foreign Debt and Nigeria's Economic Development, Lagos, March 5–6, 1984, p. 3.

2. Ibid., p. 23.

3. Ibid., p. 5.

4. Adedeji, "Foreign Debt and the Prospects of Growth"; H. Wilkens, "The Debt Burden of Developing Countries," *Economics* 28 (1983):39–48.

References

Acquah, Paul A. "Sources and Modes of Financing for Developing Nations," paper presented at Conference on Foreign Debt and Nigeria's Economic Development, Lagos, March 5–6, 1984.

Adedeji, A. "Foreign Debt and the Prospects of Growth in the Developing Countries of Africa in the 1980's," paper presented at Conference on Foreign Debt and Nigeria's Economic Development, Lagos, March 5–6, 1984.

Clausen, A. W. "Let's Not Panic About Third World Debts." *Harvard Business Review,* November-December 1983.

Hope, N., and T. Klein. *Finance and Development* 20, no. 3, September 1983.

Hughes, H. "The External Debt of Developing Countries." *Finance and Development* 14, no. 4, December 1977.

Nashashibi, K. "Devaluation in Developing Countries: The Different Choices." *Finance and Development* 20, no. 1, March 1983.

Schultz, S. "Foreign Debt of the Third World: Problems, Prospects and Possible Solutions." *Economics* 24 (1981):29–46.

Ubogu, Roland E. "Deficit Financing in Nigeria: The Experience of the 1970–1980 Decade." *Journal of Management Studies* (forthcoming).

Wilkens, H. "The Debt Burden of Developing Countries." *Economics* 24 (1983):39–48.

9

Bridging the Financial Gap: The Creative Use of Venture Capital in Africa

Jeffrey L. Jackson
TIPCO

The 1980s mark a turning point in Africa's quest for economic growth and transformation. During the previous twenty years (1960–1980), unilateral and bilateral donor agencies injected billions of dollars into Africa's new and fragile economies. The results of this huge investment are mixed. In the area of "social overhead," significant gains in literacy, health, power, and transportation will pay significant dividends in future years.

Africa's macroeconomic performance, on the other hand, has been disappointing. Although some countries have performed well—notably Nigeria, Ivory Coast, and Malawi—African countries as a group fared poorly when compared against all developing countries. Between 1970 and 1980, the GNP of developing countries as a group grew at an average annual rate of 2.7 percent; for sub-Saharan African the figure was 0.8 percent. During the 1970–1980 period, fifteen African countries recorded negative growth in per capita income, and by the end of the decade even the high-growth countries were slowing down. For the period, low-income African countries posted growth of 0.3 percent, whereas the GNP of middle-income countries fell by 0.5 percent.

An evaluation by Africa's senior finance and planning officials of Africa's lackluster economic performance led to the development of two documents, the World Bank's *Accelerated Development in Sub-Saharan Africa* (the so-called Berg Report) and the Organization for African Unity's (OAU) "Lagos Plan of Action" (LPA). Both documents were requested at the highest levels in order to provide African governments with a framework for both short- and long-term planning.

The *Accelerated Development* report dealt with policy recommendations for the short term (1981–1990), whereas the LPA laid out a long-term policy strategy (1981–2000). Though these documents differ in many respects, they share one common recommendation—that it is essential to give production a higher priority in the allocation of economic resources. Second, the documents emphasized the need to rely increasingly on private entrepreneurs and investment and less on parastatal and other government controls.

Resource Constraints

Africa is chronically short of the funds required for development, capital expenditures, and recurrent expenditures. The current shortfall in financial resources is critical given the combination of declining per capital agricultural production and export volume, dwindling official development assistance, and a steep decline in international bank lending. Multilateral and bilateral financial institutions are very effective in designing, financing, and implementing projects in the areas of physical infrastructure, agriculture, rural development, education, and health. However, there must be a shift in emphasis toward the financing of directly productive activities. This shift should not come at the expense of current levels of development assistance; rather, additional financial resources should be provided.

According to the *Accelerated Development* report:

A reordering of postindependence priorities is essential if economic growth is to accelerate. During the past two decades most African governments rightly focused on political consolidation, on the laying down of basic infrastructure (much of it tied to the goal of political integration), and on the development of human resources. *Relatively less attention was paid to production.* Now it is essential to give production a higher priority—without neglecting these other goals. Without a faster rate of production increase, other objectives cannot be achieved, nor can past achievements be sustained. (Emphasis added.)[1]

Appropriately constructed investment projects should provide a wide range of economic and financial benefits: job creation/retention, increased income, increased tax revenues, additional foreign exchange, and increased utilization of domestic raw materials.

Current global economic conditions are exacerbating Africa's already declining resource balance. The aggregate resource balance in Africa (the difference between exports and imports of goods and nonfactor services) appears to be unchanged between 1960 and 1979. However, this statistic masks the disproportionate weight given to oil-exporting countries, which fared well over the period. As a group they improved markedly from a gap of −6 percent in 1960 to +1 percent in 1979. On the other hand, for low-income countries the gap grew from −2 percent to −9 percent, whereas middle-income oil importers retreated from relative balance in 1960 to a gap of −4 percent in 1979. The implications of a continuing resource gap are that individual countries will not be able to finance required levels of imports, debt, and domestic capital formation, whether public or private.

The resource imbalance is compounded by the prospective decline in net capital inflows from $10.8 billion (annual average 1980–82) to $5 billion (projected, annual average 1985–87). This dramatic decline in financial resources comes at a critical point in Africa's development and is inconsistent with multilateral agencies' program of action and the need for reorientation of policies. An analysis of Table 9.1 reveals the problem areas: (1) Net private capital inflows decline to an annual average of minus $1 billion as a result of a substantial rise in amortization (loan payments) and a small decline in capital inflows; and (2) net capital flows resulting from bilateral and multilateral loans and grants diminish by $2.3 billion.

In spite of these disparaging statistics a resource gap and the diminution of capital flows are not sufficient reasons for the apparent shortage of capital for investment projects. A frequently mentioned observation relative to expanded private sector activity in Africa is that there are sufficient loanable funds but there is not an adequate supply of sound bankable projects. At the same time, a number of potentially profitable investment projects are not going forward. A plausible explanation for this imbalance is a shortage of resources available for the technical and financial preparation of prospective projects. Whereas small businesspeople in developing countries often lack the experience and knowledge to prepare sophisticated business and financial plans, commercial banks and other lenders—which have the capability—are not staffed to take over the job of project preparation, which for smaller projects is likely to be prohibitively costly. Undoubtedly, if sounder investment projects were developed, financial institutions would make funds available.

Private Foreign Investment

African nations need immediate and sustained capital inflows. Thus the issue is not whether additional capital is required but rather how it can be applied and on what terms it can be obtained. The current strategy being pushed, principally by the United States, is that the

Table 9.1 Sub-Saharan Africa: External Capital Flows, 1980-1982 and
1985-1987 (current US$ billion)

	1980-1982 annual average (estimates)	1985-1987 annual average (projection in the absence of special action)
Total		
Gross capital flows	13.1	13
Amortization	2.3	8
Net capital flows	10.8	5
Private		
Gross capital flows	4.2	4
Amortization	1.7	5
Net capital flows	2.5	-1
Bilateral and multilateral grants and loans		
Gross capital flows	8.9	9
Amortization	0.6	3
Net capital flows	8.3	6

Note: All figures exclude use of IMF resources and repurchases. Net use of
IMF resources was, on average, $0.8 billion annually during 1980-1982.
Repurchases during 1985-1987 are estimated to be about $1 billion annually.

Source: World Bank, Accelerated Development in Sub-Sahara Africa
(Washington, D.C.: World Bank, 1982).

productive sector, i.e., the private sector, must be given an enlarged role in the allocation of increasingly scarce financial resources. At the insistence of the United States, multilateral agencies—notably the World Bank—will devote additional resources to stimulate private sector production.

The success of this approach will require that substantial policy changes be made by nearly all African governments in both practical and legal contexts.

The United States and the World Bank are willing to foster this process by supporting policy-based loans and programs that emphasize reliance on price mechanisms to encourage efficiency in resource allocation and production. For example, loans to parastatals may not go forward because such institutions are "generically inefficient." In support of the World Bank's new emphasis and program of action, one official stated, "Africa does not have even five years. The declining per capita output can not be sustained either politically or socially."

Notwithstanding the emphasis on private sector development, private foreign investment will be difficult to attract to Africa, not only because of the deteriorating economic condition but also because of Africa's poor image in the investment community. Political instability, corruption, and chronic foreign exchange shortages are only a few of the complaints voiced by investors.

The U.S. Department of State commissioned a study on obstacles to private sector activities in Africa. The study concluded:

> Having stated the drawbacks, it is important to note that the picture is not all gloomy. There are solid reasons for being optimistic about the prospects of a well-organized and balanced private sector strategy. First, a dialogue with African leaders on economic policies has begun, stimulated in large part by the World Bank, the IMF, and bilateral donors. Secondly, many African governments are actively seeking Western trade and investment, including a number of states which had heretofore been hostile to foreign private enterprise. Third, the political climate in Africa has changed, with a notable decline in the stridency and orthodoxy with which ideological principles are promoted. Finally, there have been some notable breakthroughs and successes in indigenous training programs, investment projects, and in efforts to promote policy reform. Provided there is a political commitment to go forward, there is reason to believe that real progress can be made.[2]

Private Venture Capital

Unlike private foreign investment, which often involves multinational enterprises, majority ownership, and corporate recognition, venture capitalists can inject funds into a project with few of the negative side effects. They have the flexibility of structuring an equity investment or developing loan packages to fit particular business circumstances. Venture capitalists work in partnership with the project owners and may assume 25 percent to 30 percent or less of the business equity. There is no organized international venture capital industry. However, the following description of the U.S. industry will be helpful in understanding the role and structure of venture capital.

The U.S. Venture Capital Industry

The venture capital industry in the United States consists of roughly 600 companies and identifiable individuals who have established a pattern of continuous professional interest in private transactions. The companies fall into the following categories:

- venture capital corporations
- partnership with institutional ownership

- family venture capital partnerships
- small business investment companies (SBIC)
- corporate venture divisions
- venture capital affiliates of investment banking firms
- minority enterprise SBICs (MESBIC)

MESBICs and SBICs are licensed and regulated by the U.S. Small Business Administration and are specifically prohibited from participating in overseas investment projects. The other types of venture operations can participate in overseas ventures where opportunities exist, except perhaps where prohibited by their bylaws or organizational charter.

Venture capital companies characterize potential investments in one of four basic stages: start-ups, first-stage financing, second-stage financing, and third-stage financing. Start-ups involve companies in the process of organizing or those that have been in business only a short time. These development stage enterprises are difficult to evaluate, and few venture capital companies pursue deals at this stage. First-stage financing involves companies that have expanded their initial capital on the prototype, developed some evidence of commercial interest in the product, evolved a going organization, perhaps acquired some pilot production equipment, and even obtained a small line of bank credit. Generally at this stage of financing the first outside capital flows in from organized venture capital sources.

Second-stage financing describes an investment in a company that is producing and shipping whose accounts receivable and inventories are building up and whose marketing expenses begin to mount. The company needs working capital and expansion capital. Although it has clearly made progress, it is probably still operating at a loss. Third-stage financing involves companies in which sales volume has increased to where they are breaking even or making a profit. Funds are needed for further plant expansion, marketing, working capital, or perhaps acquisitions.

The Application of Venture Capital in Africa

The ideal venture capital firm operating in the African environment will apply its efforts and capital to investment projects in the range of $500,000 to $4 to $5 million. However, this does not rule out smaller projects, particularly in the smaller countries, where projects in the $250,000 to $500,000 range may be more feasible. The broadest category of proposal opportunities involves leveraging development funds already invested in potentially profit-making enterprises, with an infusion of new investment capital from the proposed fund, in close participation with local partners in each country. In such an environment, relatively small sums in specific situations may be highly productive.

The venture capital company will commit capital for a long period of time (five to seven years or more) and closely monitor projects. The staff will, in cooperation with local businesspeople and sponsors, prepare investment proposals that will include such required elements as management, technical aspects, marketing, supply of raw materials, agreements among owners, and financial plan. The venture firm will review contract arrangements affecting any of the key project elements and recommend changes where required. In developing a realistic financial plan, staff will prepare cash flow analyses, calculations of financial rates of return on the project, and deviation analysis (analyses of the sensitivity of projected income and debt servicing to possible adverse changes in costs or revenues).

Because the venture firm's capital will essentially be locked into a project for a long time, every project requires some form of oversight. Intensive monitoring, in the form of frequent progress and performance reports, is essential for the venture firm that has capital at risk to be able to identify potential problems before they develop. In selected cases, the firm may wish to have a position on a portfolio company's board of directors.

Success of venture capital companies' operations in Africa is based on the premise that there are sufficient investment opportunities in sub-Saharan Africa. Nicolas Plessez of the Organization for Economic Cooperation and Development (OECD) comments: "As it has been demonstrated by a few shrewd operators (e.g., Tiny Rowland with Lonrho), there are quite a number of enterprises with reasonable good growth prospects which can be taken over for very little money and can be expanded and made profitable with limited injections of capital and know-how. The same applies to a number of investment projects which have been abandoned at a more or less advanced stage of completion for a variety of non-economic reasons."

A secondary premise is that conditions exist for foreign investment in parastatal enterprises and other enterprises under local control. Several African countries are rethinking the role of state-owned companies and are looking at methods of increasing their efficiency. Liberia has gone so far as to privatize previously state-owned and -run enterprises. Other sub-Saharan African countries are encouraging private (though not necessarily majority) participation and management of parastatal enterprises.

Although Africa is frequently characterized as the region with the worst overall investment climate, several countries have revised their investment codes over the past few years to offer liberal investment incentives including tax concessions, free trade zones, reduction or elimination of import duties, and preferential treatment for licenses and permits and approvals.

Notwithstanding the potential benefits to be derived from the application of venture capital, there is a substantial amount of associated risk. A higher than average return on investment is therefore required. Equity/debt investments, particularly those in young rapidly growing companies, tend to be highly illiquid under any circumstances. Where no broad markets exist for reselling securities at substantially capitalized values, it is sometimes difficult to show an adequate overall return on investment even when a large portion of a portfolio is invested for current return. In addition, managing a portfolio of securities in growing concerns, especially in Africa, requires high levels of expense, which must be covered from returns before investors are paid.

Additional reservations about the concept of venture capital in Africa concern (1) African governments' commitment to making foreign-supported private sector investment profitable and safe; (2) competition with larger multilateral donors for the best investment projects; (3) the ability to find or develop indigenous management and technical skills; and (4) social, political, and infrastructure conditions.

As regards the first reservation, Niles Helmboldt, president of Equator Bank, comments:

There are a few [African] countries that are avowedly *laissez faire* in their attitude towards the marketplace, but even those countries can be jealous of national prerogatives where investment is concerned. There is a general openness towards foreign money, less openness towards foreign ownership. At the other end of the political spectrum, some of Africa's more socialistically inclined governments are now balancing revolutionary rhetoric with warm words for foreign enterprise, even going so far as to revise investment codes, but it is difficult to tell whether this change of heart is permanent or a side effect of worldwide hard times.

The true test for both kinds of governments lies in the kinds of incentives they will be willing to offer you, incentives that justify your investors' risk at the outset and confirm the governments' long term dedication to making foreign-supported enterprise workable and safe. You will have to sit down with senior government officials to hammer out terms and form your own cautious judgement about the strength of that dedication. Venture capital companies must be positioned carefully vis-a-vis multilateral donor agencies. As a noted banker accurately points out, " . . . there is one area where their interest and support seems to be increasing, and that is in the area of providing capital to small and medium-scale business. It will be difficult for a new private investment bank to make sound, profitable loans in the face of competition from international aid agencies." However, if feasible and well-defined, the financial role of venture capital could complement the activities of—and even work in tandem with—such institutions as the World Bank, the Arab Bank for African Development, OPIC, AID and the OPEC Fund for International Development, among others.

The reservations concerning the lack of management/technical skills and undeveloped infrastructure will vary significantly from country to country and within countries from sector to sector. Indeed there are now places in Africa with large pools of educated managers and technicians. Viewed continentwide however, an acute shortage is readily apparent. One critical task will be, on a case-by-case basis, to address, circumvent, or avoid this problem. Infrastructure poses a more manageable type of problem since its extent and limitations are known factors and can be factored into project costs before any commitment of funds.

Having discussed these principal reservations concerning the development and operation of venture capital companies in Africa, I must note that despite these reservations and risks a number of investment projects are going forward. Private foreign investors are committing capital and obtaining a return on investments in African companies: A respondent to a 1982 survey conducted by the U.S. State Department indicates:

> The best countries to invest in are obviously those in which you can get the best return on investment. It varies from place to place, but generally 20 percent return on investment is what we look for because of the high risk factor in Africa. Unless it is a large project we look for a four year payout. We expect the government to participate; that means they have a commitment to the project.[3]

This strategy captures an emerging consensus in development finance, relating to the use of private mechanisms. Dunstan Wai, a noted Africanist now at the World Bank, states that "many African countries are beginning to realize that more efficient use of scarce resources is essential to the development process, and moreover, the stringent circumstances facing the world economy for the next few years will require more reliance on the private sector and less on official development assistance."[4]

Conclusion

The venture capital concept is already being exploited by the so-called niche bankers. These bankers are part of a relatively new breed of "specialized financial engineers"—usually small firms with extensive expertise in certain regions. These niche banks do not tackle mega-projects. Rather, they generally participate in deals in the $500,000 to $50 million range in sectors such as telecommunications, trucking, construction, food processing, tourism, and small-scale energy. According to Carl Bazarian, managing director of the East-West Group, "the philosophy is that in seemingly unbankable countries there *are* bankable deals."

Creative financing is the hallmark of these firms. Although financing occasionally involves such classic sources as the commercial banks and traditional capital markets, niche bankers frequently rely on creative combinations of venture capital, collateral, and export credits from official export credit agencies. Instead of taking dominant positions in projects, they team up with outside entities such as regional development banks and private investors to support the project. The Nassau-based Equator Bank, which operates predominately in Africa, tends to take a 100 percent share of most projects. It minimizes risk through export insurance and government guarantees.

A recent article in the financial magazine, *Institutional Investor,* succinctly defines the role to be played by niche banks and venture capital: "With the market in syndicated loans to sovereign borrowers at such a low ebb, many niche bankers extol the virtues of increased exposure via project finance as the way eventually to pump up languishing debtor economies. 'Banks will have to find new ways to support projects that not only pay their own way,' concludes Equator Bank's Helmboldt, 'but that will eventually generate a surplus to help pay off the old financings.'"

The eventual role that venture capital will play in Africa depends less on the immediate economic situation than on the policy and business environments. There are bankable projects waiting to be developed and financed. Appropriately selected and financed projects can have an economic impact far greater than the simple blunt infusion of capital. In the almost certain absence of other private capital over the next few years, venture capital is an option that must be taken seriously.

Notes

1. World Bank, *Accelerated Development in Sub-Saharan Africa* (Washington, D.C.: World Bank, 1982), pp. 4–5.

2. Pauline Baker, *Obstacles to Private Sector Activities in Africa* (Washington, D.C.: U.S. Department of State, Bureau of Intelligence and Research, 1983), p. 81.

3. Ibid., p. 31.

4. Dr. Wai is the assistant to the regional vice-president, eastern and southern African regions, World Bank. Dr. Wai's remarks were made during the conference upon which this book is based.

10

The Local Private Sector and Socialism in Algeria

Hocine Benissad
University of Algiers

Since 1962 socialist Algeria has been trying to set up a framework for the development of the nonagricultural private sector. However, the nationalization of foreign firms (and even those of Algerians) and bureaucratic controls encircling private production have discouraged private initiative and have lead to considerable hoarding of money and capital flight through parallel exchange markets.

The Legislative Framework

Two stages must be distinguished in the development of the Algerian private sector. Up to 1979, this sector had been in retreat because of the populist discourse that prevailed, which denounced all "forms of domestic or foreign exploitation." Since 1979–1980 the public powers have been attempting to reassure and stimulate private initiative and to grapple with the flaws of the public sector.

Withdrawal of the Private Sector (1962–1980)

The setting up of new political institutions and attempts to resume disrupted economic activities right after independence absorbed all the efforts of the state. The government did not hesitate to request the private sector to participate in the construction of the national economy. To remedy the climate of instability that prevailed at the time, to halt the flight of capital abroad (especially to France), and to encourage the acquisition of national capital, a law on private investments was enacted on July 26, 1963. This law attempted to reassure foreign investors by granting them guarantees and access to financial facilities.

97

The supreme guarantee offered then by the state remains today—a safeguard for foreign capital against nationalization. Nationalization may occur, according to this law, only "when the amount of accrued net profits will have reached the sum of invested foreign capital."

Financial incentives consisted of total or partial exemption from taxes and duties, reimbursement of production tax on the purchase of equipment, protection against foreign competition, and so on. But the foreign investor then and still today remained reluctant to invest in Algeria.

The change of government that occurred three years after independence led the Revolutionary Council to redefine its position toward the private sector in the declaration of July 5, 1965. This statement invited the national capitalist sector to participate in the construction of a modern and integrated economy, recognized "the necessity to use national resources in order to speed up economic independence," and "considered national savings and investments as important contributions to the building of the nation." According to the Revolutionary Council, "it is advisable, however, to orient investments towards profitable and productive economic activities with linkage effects, and not to confine them to speculative or unproductive activities." In this new context, on September 15, 1966, an investment code was promulgated for the national holders of capital. This code fixed the principles governing private sector investments, which now required the consent of the state. It outlined the framework for the intervention of private capital in the development of productive nonagricultural sectors (especially industry and tourism). Generally, national or foreign private investment is unrestricted in the nonstrategic areas. In the key sectors reserved for the public sector, the state can have national or foreign private capital participate by means of a joint venture. Furthermore the state at all times has the power to "redeem all or part of the shares of which it is not the owner," in all private companies, approved or nonapproved. Such a takeover (with compensation according to law) may be justified by an imperative as vague as that of "economic development."

The basic guarantee concerns compensation for authorized private investments: The Investment Code states that in case the public interest demands nationalization, such a measure could only be brought about by a legislative decree and the payment of compensation (equal to the fixed net value after an appraisal by experts, increased by the amount of depreciation and of interest at the same rate for a period of two years) must be made within nine months. This compensation is transferable if the beneficiary is a foreigner and if the investment has been made by means of foreign capital brought into Algeria. Private firms have the right to recruit foreign skilled personnel within authorized limits. Foreign firms are equal before the law and have the right to transfer net profits up to 15 percent of the amount of their contribution to added value or of liquidation and loans contracted abroad. The financial benefits allowed by the Algerian Investment Code are of the same nature as those granted in liberal economies; it allows the total or partial exemption from the costly right of legal transfer and from land taxes fixed in terms of geographical location, the reduction of production taxes, and so on. Nevertheless, other barriers posed by the state—the difficulties in getting machines and raw materials, the stiffness of fiscal controls and many unfavorable prejudices experienced by the private sector in Algeria—slowed down its rate of investment in 1967–1981.

The Investment Code itself is not an exacting and rigorous regulation of the private sector. Contrary to public investments, private investments are not subjected to any planning, leaving the field free for the spirit of initiative of the private sector from which the state expects in return a contribution to national development. The granting of benefits could have permitted more extensive regulations of private investments and subjected them to medium- and long-term planning (location, professional training, integration).

Current Orientations

At the end of December 1981, the Central Committee of the Party,[1] dealing especially with private sector legal documents, stresses its "appreciable contribution to national production and the satisfaction of certain social needs" and its "complementary and nonantagonistic character with regard to the public sector." However, as there has been an "absence of a clear policy as regards the private sector," it declares as necessary:

1. To "outline positive possibilities for private businesses and to assure them appropriate guarantees in order to better mobilize their services for national development."
2. To set up "a national authority responsible for the orientation, stimulation, and coordination of investments in the private sector"; this authority would ensure the "control" of the size of the firms of the private sector (via profit immobilizations, etc.) and their security against nationalization.
3. To transform tax policy into an "essential instrument of income policy in the private sector" and "direction of investments" in this sector.

4. To revise laws directing the organization and management of the state monopoly on foreign trade in order to improve the provision of supplies "in favour of all the sectors of the national economy."
5. To "strengthen" the dialogue with private investors, to work with them to improve and simplify the procedures of authorization of projects.
6. To involve the "operators of the national private sector . . . in the identification and solution of their problems."

This is clear evidence of a new state attitude vis-à-vis the private sector. The attitude has shifted to an active and nondiscriminatory national private investment policy; that is, previous unfavorable prejudices that used to hurt the private, independent productive sector are supposed to give way to political guarantees, securities on supplies of inputs and capital equipment, and increased aid from banks and other technical organizations. A law was promulgated in 1982 on the code on national private investments. Generally, it takes up the dispositions of 1966 code while placing new stress on the need to channel private domestic savings toward investments in small and medium-scale industry, in fishing, construction, public works, and transports, and finally, in social services.

Henceforth, all the sectors are thus in principle open to private entrepreneurs to whom special benefits are granted with the following provisions:

- They orient themselves toward the so-called underprivileged regions, like "Aures" and the South.
- They mobilize their currency by proper means to finance purchases of capital equipment.
- They successfully export locally produced goods.

In January 1983, a board responsible for the stimulation and coordination of the private sector was set up; it is an administrative organization with (for the time being) limited resources. Its objective consists mainly in giving prior approval to every document submitted to the commissions responsible for private investments. The faithful application of this code and procedure should allow an increase in the extent to which liberal precepts affect the Algerian economy. This liberalism will of course be only relative, since the Central Committee still supports "the construction of a dominant socialist sector in the national economy." Although in the official ideology attempts have been made since 1980 to rehabilitate the private sector and to encourage its growth, the central regulatory texts and bureaucratic practices have not greatly changed. To illustrate this institutional rigidity we can say: Investors who buy capital equipment abroad with their own foreign currencies are encouraged whereas the acquisition of foreign currencies by residents on the black market is a serious offence against exchange control regulations; and the banking system remains stingy in granting the private sector operating loans and capital credits.

Nevertheless, the present ideological choice is in favor of encouraging and extending the private sector (especially small and medium-scale industry), in spite of apparent resistance shown by divisions of the state bureaucracy (which benefit from state intervention). In other words, we may conclude that the efforts to collectivize the Algerian economy have leveled off.

It is in this context that in May 1987 the national secretary of the FLN party declared to the French newspaper *L'Humanite:*

> In the absence of institutions the truth is that during the previous two decades we were afraid of the private sector and the collaboration with the foreign firms. Therefore we took severe steps in this field. . . . But nowadays after the 4th and 5th Congresses of the FLN Party, after the institutions building up, we think that, given present laws, regulations, managers, and structures, our institutions can collaborate with national and foreign private sector without fear or complex. This is a reality imposed by the national economy evolution and the new changing relations in the world.

The Importance of the Private Sector

At the close of the 1970s, the private sector contributed about 42 percent of industrial value-added (if we leave out the hydrocarbon sector). It now consists of companies employing 5 to 1,000 workers, with a turnover ranging from 200,000 to 50 million DA (Algerian dinars) (5.1 DA 1984 = US$1), and whose fixed capital may be up to 50 million DA. According to a survey of the National Institute of Productivity and Development, the private sector controls about one-third of the production of capital goods and about two-thirds of consumer goods. In certain areas of production, it dominates, producing 100 percent of synthetic leathers, 75 percent of shoes, and 75 percent of the country's textile products. Statistics given by the Ministry of Planning of Algeria on the private sector share in industrial output in 1978 indicate the importance of the private companies in national output:

	Million DA	%
Hydrocarbons	2,433	22.1
Industry	4,161	16.9
Construction and public works	2,590	19.0

As regards employment, the private industrial sector is also quite important though its share in total employment by branch is not as high as its share in production. But this is explained by the difference between the criteria for recruitment in the private and public sectors. Six remarks can be made about the private industrial sector on this point. First, it subscribes to the most profitable short-term productive activities (textiles, poultry, confectionaries). Second, it is concentrated geographically in and around the three largest towns (Algiers, Constantine, and Oran), which account for (according to the survey of the National Institute of Productivity and Development) 60 percent of the private industrial companies. Certain towns still attract activities for which they have a comparative advantage, for example, textiles in Tizi-Duzou and Tlemcen, leather and hide in Medea and El-Asnam. Private entrepreneurs seem to avoid the poorer regions.

Third, private sector companies avoid asking the consent of the Investment Commissions because of inadequate functioning of the latter and of the general tendency to finance their own investments; according to statistical figures of the Algerian Development Bank, the amount of projects registered by these commissions is not more than 860 million DA in the period 1966–1974. Fourth, in 1966–1973, the private sector created 23,000 jobs of which about 15,000 were created in 1970 alone. A slowdown in the development of the private industrial sector occurred between 1971 and 1980 largely because of the rapid extension of the collectivization of the national economy beginning in 1971. According to the Algerian Development Bank, 1980 employment in the private industrial sector was as follows:

Industrial processing	104,002
Other industries	2,281
Construction and public works	126,486
Total	232,769

Fifth, although the National Charter, adopted in 1976, affirms the right of the productive nonexploiting private sector to exist and function (when it does not threaten socialism) no resumption of private investments was noticed in 1976–1982. Sixth, the industrial private sector is very dependent on its external economic environment and in particular on the public enterprises endowed with monopolies in foreign trade, giving them access to imported goods and capital equipment. This dependence was confirmed during the adoption of the law on state monopoly in foreign trade (early 1978) that for a while plunged the private sector into crisis arising from an interruption of the supply of important imports. Furthermore, because the sector has to make all its purchases in cash private sector firms can survive only if they are highly liquid.

The public sector—broad-based and politically powerful—offers the private domestic sector, which is small and devoid of real political power, many opportunities for expansion. On this point, M. A. Ben-achenehou has developed some interesting, though contestable, ideas. Roughly, he maintains that:

1. The private sector is developing "downstream" from the public sector. The public sector produces inputs with very costly investments, long periods of maturity, and complex technologies and then sells them to the private sector that processes them, turning them into finished products.
2. The private sector buys these inputs at controlled price and sells its finished products at more or less illicit prices, within oligopolistic or even monopolistic market structures; its profits therefore result in organized inflation, diversion of public savings, poor working conditions, poor quality of products and services.
3. The private sector benefits from the increase in demand induced by public investment programs (for instance in construction) and specializes in activities that involve considerable financing, sophisticated technology, and uncertain profitability for the public sector. These activities are those in which increase in prices is the fastest and in which profit margins are the least controlled.

However, Benachenehou, in asking about the "social destination" of public industrial production, does not recall that in all mixed economies (whose virtues he denies) industrial specialization in the private and public sectors is similar to that prevailing in Algeria. In many economies, investments in basic industries are made by the public sector. According to Peter Evans, in Brazil the closer the industrial activity gets to final consumption the more dominant is the control of firms by the private sector, whether national or foreign.[2] In Algeria, the increased specialization of the private industrial sector is inhibited by the institution of state monopolies of import, which greatly reduce the scope of private investment.

If we understand that the private sector in Algeria operates downstream from the public sector—largely because of laws that give state corporations a monopoly on all external contacts and trade—then arguments about the exploitative character of the private sector must be reconsidered. A. Khellaf, for instance, writes that to allow "the national private sector to embark on a course of large scale industrialization amounts to helping the national bourgeoisie to develop relations with foreign capitalism and at the same time open the way to imperialism and political dependency."[3] It must be noted, however, that given the persistence of the state monopoly on foreign trade, direct contacts between the national private sector and foreign firms are difficult or impossible. The choice of production instruments and negotiations on the conditions for their acquisition are always the prerogative of the public enterprises, even if these instruments are destined for the private sector. The real risk of "exploition" would seem to emerge from the relationship between foreign firms and the technocracy of the Algerian public sector.

However, these ideological quarrels cannot obscure the main point: Everyone now agrees that a larger, more productive private sector would greatly increase the flexibility and adaptability of the Algerian economy, which to date has been dominated by a system of state monopolies.

Notes

1. Algeria has a centralized government and a simple political party. Since 1979 the government has administered the country, taking its guidance on fundamental policy issues from periodic congresses of the National Liberation Front party and from the party's Central Committee between congresses.

2. P. Evans, "Multinationals, State-Owned Corporations, and the Transformation of Imperialism: A Brazilian Case Study," *Economic Development and Cultural Change* 26, no. 1 (October 1977):58.

3. A. Khellaf, director general of planning and industrial development at the Ministry of Industry and Energy, paper presented at the First Congress of Economists of the Third World, February 1976, Algiers.

11

State and Structural Influences on Private Initiative: An East Asian Case

Paul W. Kuznets
Department of Economics,
Indiana University

Interest in the role of private initiative in economic development and, in particular, in the innovating function of the entrepreneur, can be traced to Joseph Schumpeter's *The Theory of Economic Development*, first published in 1911. The role of private initiative is still of interest today, especially as it conflicts with public or social initiative, and will undoubtedly continue to be a matter of concern since the conflict is based on moral and political as well as economic considerations and is therefore difficult to resolve. Though constraints on private initiative or incentives that promote private initiative may be constraints or incentives for entrepreneurs, private initiative transcends entrepreneurship so that such constraints or incentives may affect consumption, saving, or work efforts of economic agents who are not entrepreneurs. Constraints on the import of consumer goods, for instance, limit consumer choice; higher interest rates provide an incentive for private saving; an increase in job openings is likely to expand labor force participation.

The main concern here is private initiative as it affects individuals in their economic roles as producers, whether entrepreneurs or not, and in particular the public (state) and structural influences on private initiative. "Structural" is not used to denote traditional or historic factors as distinct from the economic-institutional framework and the international environment (possible exogenous and endogenous constraints and incentives) as it was in Workshops I and II. Rather "structural" is used to denote factors that affect private initiative that are not amenable to short-run policy manipulation, such as the economic-institutional framework or dependence on foreign trade. These are "structural" in my sense because they define the pace and character of development, because they change slowly if at all, and because they have to change for development to accelerate and/or for the benefits of development to be distributed differently.

Because our colloquium focuses on constraints and incentives in Africa, there is a question of why this chapter deals with an East Asian case—South Korea, or the Republic of Korea. Korea is the largest member of the so-called Gang of Four (the others are Taiwan, Hong Kong, and Singapore), East Asian countries distinguished by their combination of rapid growth and unusually equal income distributions. Because the East Asian case is one of successful economic development, it should provide a useful model or paradigm for examining the factors that impinge on private initiative in Africa. The paradigm must be used selectively, however, to be instructive. Though there are obvious similarities, in that Korea shares a colonial inheritance with most African nations and not so long ago would have been included with most African countries in the World Bank's low or lower-middle income categories, there are important differences that should not be ignored. These are mainly social, cultural, and political rather than economic differences, however, so the proximate incentives and constraints that bear on the development of private initiative in Korea should be similar to those that operate among African nations, even if the underlying incentives and constraints are not similar.

The applicability or inapplicability of the Korean model should become apparent to readers familiar with African development in the next two sections of this chapter. The first examines demand considerations that might promote or limit private initiative, particularly the size of the public sector, the extent of government intervention in the economy, and the adequacy of domestic markets. The second section evaluates supply-side factors such as investment in human and physical capital and the acquisition of technological capabilities. Successes, failures, continuing problems, and future prospects for private initiative are considered in the third and concluding section.

The Scope of Private Initiative

Private initiative, like specialization, is limited by the size of the market, where market size is defined by the output of privately produced goods and services. Private initiative should have greater play, *ceteris paribus:* the larger the share of private output, the smaller the share of public output in total output. The most straightforward way to estimate the size of the private market would be to find GDP or GNP originating in the private sector, but this would be misleading in Korea because accounts of state-owned enterprises (SOEs) such as the tobacco monopoly and KEPCO (the Korea Electric Power Company) are included in the private sector and not, as is the practice elsewhere, in the public sector. Possible proxies, clearly flawed for present purposes, are private expenditures or private claims on resources, which can be derived by subtracting government expenditure or government revenues, respectively, from GNP or GDP (the two are much the same in Korea). Each measure yields a private sector accounting for 79 percent of GNP in 1981–1982, but this figure is too high because it includes SOE output. Independent information on SOEs shows a slight decline in the share of SOE output in GDP since the 1960s, but the latest figures I could find indicate that SOEs still accounted for 8 to 9 percent of GDP by 1975–1977.[1] If we assume a continued decline to 7 percent in the last few years, then the share of GNP originating in the public sector has been around 28 percent during the early 1980s, which leaves 72 percent for the private sector.

Fragmentary and indirect data on public shares of total output in other countries indicate that the public share of the Korean market is below the international average. World Bank estimates for public consumption as a proportion of GDP show, for example, that public consumption takes up less of Korean GDP than it does in most other upper-middle-income or in African countries. Shares of SOEs in GDP were somewhat below the 10 percent average for developing countries in 1980 and well below SOE shares in Zambia, Ghana, Guinea, Tanzania, Togo, and the Ivory Coast.[2]

Even though the government supports an unusually large army, and though public enterprises are cost efficient and therefore do not drain the public fiscal reserves as in many developing countries, the relatively small size of the public sector is not surprising. It is small, though the country inherited a swollen bureaucracy and military establishment at the end of the Korean War, because these have grown little in subsequent years. Also, successive regimes under Presidents Syngman Rhee (1948–1960), Chang Myon (1960–1961), Park Chung-Hee (1961–1979), and Chun Doo-Hwan (1980 to date) have maintained a production-first philosophy that, like Japan's, has directed resources toward increasing output rather than toward meeting social goals. Output expansion, unlike social programs, does not necessarily require government outlays. The paucity of social expenditure is revealed in recent budgets, in which less than 10 percent of total outlays have been allocated to social-expenditure categories such as social security, welfare, housing, and community services.

Although a small public sector should provide more than usual scope for private initiative, it may not for two reasons. First, the public sector may be too small to finance infrastructure or to otherwise support the private sector, as was evidently the case in nineteenth-century China.[3] Second, whatever its size the government may play an active, interventionist role in the economy, as it does in Korea. This is likely to restrict private initiative, though it need not if intervention serves to improve market functions or increase economic opportunity rather than limit market entry or otherwise curb private efforts. Since state action may promote or restrict private initiative, a more laissez-faire public stance would not necessarily increase the scope of private initiative. Economists can indulge in counterfactual speculation, but they cannot rerun the Korean experience to determine whether less active governments would have done more to expand private initiative. It seems more worthwhile, therefore, to avoid the question of how private initiative would have fared in other circumstances and instead to examine the evidence of intervention, the reasons for intervention, the methods used to intervene, and the consequences of intervention for private initiative.

Evidence abounds that the Park and Chun regimes have played active roles in economic affairs. For example, the list of items eligible for import, the terms of export financing, and the tax-rate maxima are changed frequently. Besides the usual repertoire of monetary, fiscal, and commercial policy instruments, Korean governments have used other means to achieve economic ends. They ration credit, regulate foreign capital inducement, and generally do not hesitate to intervene directly in markets. After the second oil shock and disastrous harvest of 1980, for instance, the Chun regime used wage and price controls to curb inflation; both the Park and Chun regimes have employed a "two-price" policy to increase farmers' incomes and reduce urban rice costs.

Concern here is primarily with intervention during the past two decades (under the Park and Chun regimes) because Korea's outstanding economic success began only in the mid-1960s. Also, the preceding Chang government was in office too briefly to accomplish much, whereas the attentions of the earlier Rhee regime were absorbed by threats to its political survival rather than by economic matters. It was sufficiently concerned with the economic situation, however, to inaugurate the same import substitution strategy adopted by most developing countries after independence to establish a domestic industrial base, a process Benjamin Cohen and Gustav Ranis have termed the "first postwar restructuring."[4] And, as elsewhere, this import substitution strategy eventually succumbed to inflation, overvalued exchange rates, import restrictions, heavy trade deficits, and the other byproducts of inept policy and weak implementation. The situation changed in the mid-1960s under the Park government when it became apparent that Rhee's economic strategy was bankrupt, that U.S. assistance was to be phased out, and that better economic performance was needed if the new regime, which came to power by military coup in 1961, was to acquire political legitimacy. Change was marked, as elsewhere, by devaluation, import liberalization, a general relaxation of controls, and a series of measures designed to expand exports, all features of Cohen and Ranis' "second restructuring." The result was a sharp acceleration in the pace of economic growth and continued high levels of expansion to this day.

Change was possible under the Park regime because the factors that might conceivably permit government intervention in the economy were favorable. Stagnation during the late 1950s and the early 1960s invited drastic measures to improve economic performance. Also, a set of deeply rooted national characteristics made intervention feasible. These include Korea's hierarchic and authoritarian Confucian tradition that governs family and political relations and a history of highly centralized government consistent with Confucian tradition. Population (now around 40 million) was small enough, unlike China's, to administer readily, whereas land area (98,000 square kilometers) is compact, unlike Indonesia's. In addition, since Korea's population is unusually homogeneous, there are no ethnic or linguistic minorities with separatist interests or claims for special treatment. Furthermore, the threat of attack from the north has had a powerful unifying effect.

Other factors that encouraged government intervention have been the primacy of economic goals, effective administration, and the "psychology of success." Great emphasis by the Korean media on economic matters, insofar as media coverage reflects public priorities, can be taken as evidence of the unusually high priority attached to economic goals. While preservation of political power and maintenance of national security are important goals in Korea as elsewhere, the economic failures of previous governments and the utility of good economic performance in providing political legitimacy for new military regimes have raised the status of economic goals under Presidents Park and Chun.

Administration has been effective because political leaders have been able to use the apparatus of government to transmit and enforce their policy directives. Unlike Gunner Myrdal's "soft states" of South Asia where "policies decided on are often not enforced" and where "the authorities . . . are reluctant to place obligations on people," Korea is a "hard state" where the regime has been able to obtain compliance with government directives either by direct command or through discretionary controls.[5] The efficacy of direct command under military, bureaucratic-authoritarian regimes such as the Park and Chun regimes is self-evident.[6] Discretionary controls, in turn, work because the leadership's commitment to economic goals is passed down through the hierarchical command structure to the lowest administrative levels so that no official can afford to act in ways that might obstruct this commitment.[7]

The "psychology of success" refers to target achievement by interventionist regimes which, because they have succeeded in meeting economic goals through intervention, intervene again when the occasion arises. Successful intervention, in short, has fostered further intervention whereas unsuccessful intervention would not have. Other possibilities suggested by Korean experience—that the Park and Chun regimes have intervened because they are authoritarian regimes or that they have been successful because they are authoritarian—can be dismissed. There is no a priori reason why authoritarian regimes should be more active in economic affairs than democratic regimes, whereas the possibility that success follows from authoritarianism is contradicted by evidence that there is no correlation between economic success and type of regime, though countries with "authoritarian forms of government [tend to] perform either very well or very poorly."[8]

Intervention takes many forms in Korea, but three of these—planning, credit allocation, and export-promotion measures—merit particular attention. Planning is especially controversial because it is not evident what Korean planning accomplishes; some view it as a means for improving market functions whereas others come close to attributing Korea's success to planning. Though there is a large market-oriented private sector not bound by the plans, planning is more prescriptive than in Japan, for example, because the government tends to intervene more, particularly in allocating credit. On the other hand, since actual growth has typically outrun plan targets, plans tend to become increasingly irrelevant with time. Since planning elsewhere has not always met with economic success, what is significant in Korea is probably the combination of planning and effective policy implementation.[9]

Credit allocation, the main instrument of government intervention, is effective because the typical enterprise is highly leveraged and therefore particularly vulnerable to reduction or withdrawal of credit. The government directs special purpose banks, supervises commercial banks through the Monetary Board, and controls access to foreign credit through Exchange Bank guarantees on foreign loans. Since loanable funds are scarce and lending rates are limited by statute, the organized money market (the banking system) cannot fully satisfy the demand for credit. This leaves the unorganized money market (curb market) to meet excess demand, usually at a cost of two to four times the going rates at banks. Since excess demand requires rationing, credit is allocated in ways that suit government goals. Allocation in recent years has therefore favored export activity, heavy and chemical industry projects, and the *chaebol* (large conglomerate enterprises).

Export promotion measures are significant in Korea because the government places unbelievable emphasis on expanding exports. Export targets have been set and monthly national trade-promotion meetings held to inform firms of new priorities and evaluate reasons for discrepancies between actual and targeted performance. On Export Day each year individuals and firms are given awards for outstanding performance. Great ingenuity has been lavished on other measures to encourage exports, such as tax exemption, an import-link system (which permits exporters to obtain otherwise prohibited imports for incorporation in exports), import licensing (only firms meeting some export minimum are licensed to import), and "leakage" (standard breakage allowances are large enough so that exporters can profit from sales of export goods at high prices on the domestic market). Most important is favored access to credit. The goal is to alter incentives facing entrepreneurs so that they will find export sales as profitable or more profitable than domestic sales. Estimates of effective protection (on domestic sales) and subsidy rates (on exports) indicate that exports have, in fact, been more profitable, and this is one reason why exports have increased from insignificant levels in the early 1960s to $24 billion in 1983 and now account for around 40 percent of GNP and 25 percent of total value-added.[10]

Planning, credit allocation, and export promotion policies are major if not necessarily representative instruments of government intervention that illustrate how intervention can promote or constrain private initiative. Insofar as planning requires forecasts of future expansion by sector and industry and typically includes a project list, planning should facilitate private initiative by reducing information costs, risk, and uncertainty. The plans' emphasis on growth also generates an expansionary psychology that, by encouraging private investment, has usually proved self-fulfilling. In addition, planning might attract foreign financing to public projects that would otherwise be available for private uses, but this seems unlikely since much of the foreign capital provided to finance public sector projects comes from official sources that would not necessarily be available to finance private projects.

Credit allocation clearly constrains private initiative, unlike planning. Credit has been allocated in ways that favor public rather than private investment and, when allocated to private borrowers, has often been coupled with restrictions on market entry. Credit is typically provided to firms with the best prospects for success, so that the *chaebol* have received a disproportionate share of private sector credit while smaller firms have been starved for funds. Also, interest rate determination by the Monetary Board restricts bank initiative, even if it promotes private, curb-market activity. Furthermore, artificially low interest rate ceilings have probably reduced the total supply of credit. The curb-market portion is constrained by high risks (since curb-market activity is illegal, curb-market lenders cannot use the courts to enforce their loan agreements), while the organized-market portion is less than it would be if rates were freed to equilibrate supply and demand.

Export promotion measures offset the market distortion created by the import controls used to protect fledgling import substitution industries. Export promotion has therefore redirected private initiative from profiting by protection or by avoiding import controls to profiting by export production. Recent charges by U.S. producers that Korean exporters have been dumping in the United States suggest that the exporters have been selling below cost, possibly because of government pressure to expand exports. Cost in this instance is taken as the domestic selling price less customary markups. Since domestic prices are still artificially high because of continued protection, I suspect that the exporters may not be dumping but rather are acting in classic fashion as bilateral monopolists who maximize profit by limiting sales in the domestic market and expanding sales in export markets to benefit from the declining costs associated with economies of scale. It follows that promotion measures, rather than restricting private initiative by forcing producers to sell below cost, have encouraged private initiative as export growth has expanded the size of the markets for privately produced goods and services.

If intervention by the Park and Chun regimes has done more to promote than to constrain private initiative, it is because their economic policies have expanded GNP (and the private sector with it) more than GNP would have expanded under less interventionist regimes. The answer turns on export promotion, which has been the main theme of Korean strategy because it is the key to maximizing GNP growth by raising investment. The strategy has succeeded insofar as the investment ratio (investment/total expenditures) rose from less than 15 percent during the early 1960s to over 30 percent in some recent years. World Bank data show that investment increased more rapidly from 1960 to 1970 in Korea than in any other of the sixty-three middle-income countries in its reference group and faster from 1970 to 1980 than in all but a few oil-exporting countries. The investment has been used to expand productive capacity and therefore output, and the increase in output per unit of investment has been high (i.e., the incremental capital-output ratio has been low) because construction costs are low and investment has been concentrated in low-ratio activities. Exports are related to investment because a significant fraction of investment (25 percent in 1979–1981, for example) has been financed by borrowing from abroad. Exports generate the foreign exchange needed to repay the foreign loans while export expansion encourages foreign lenders to lend more to Korean firms because expansion promises to provide the additional foreign exchange needed to handle growing future obligations.

Cooperant Factors

Private initiative, where accepted usage of "initiative" denotes individual enterprise or the capacity to originate new ideas and methods, is the sort of individual attribute that improves economic performance and therefore should be very important for economic development. Yet, as a personal attribute or capacity, initiative is difficult to identify except after the fact and impossible to measure. Since this capacity is of little economic consequence unless individuals have the education, equipment, and the technological capability to exercise the initiative in the market place, the emphasis here is on these cooperant factors. The definition of private initiative used here includes managers and employees as well as entrepreneurs, though the entrepreneur has been the epitome of enterprise and innovation. Also, emphasis on the cooperant factors implies that private initiative is a latent characteristic and there is determined by demand rather than supply.

This last point is consistent with mainstream economists' ideas of entrepreneurship but contradicts the view held by Max Weber and Joseph Schumpeter, among others, that traditional social structures generate motivation and inhibitions that constrain private initiative. Entrepreneurship, in this view, is limited by tradition and is found mainly among socially deviant, subdominant, or threatened elite groups. Only scant evidence exists for Korea on this point; however, what little there is indicates that entrepreneurship (and, by extension, private initiative) is demand rather than supply determined.

A sample entrepreneurship survey of 311 firms in early 1976 found that entrepreneurs were not among socially deviant, subdominant, or threatened elite groups. Rather, entrepreneurs are mainly children of the wealthy pre-industrial elite (often landowners) and are extraordinarily well educated. Christians and refugees from the north are over-represented primarily because Christians are concentrated in urban areas and because a disproportionate number of refugees from the

Communist regime in the north, not surprisingly, were wealthy and well-educated members of the pre-industrial elite.[11] The combination of the low traditional status of industry and commerce and the elite background of entrepreneurs is puzzling but may follow from the weakening of traditional Confucian attitudes about business. The significant points, however, are that entrepreneurs are elite descendants of a pre-industrial elite and that entrepreneurship is less likely to be inhibited by supply than by demand considerations. This also emerges from evidence on the entrance, expansion, and exit of Korean firms. Almost three-fourths of the increase in manufacturing value-added from 1960 to 1974, for example, can be traced to the expansion of existing firms.[12] Again, the significant is not supply or the entry of new entrepreneurs but increase in the demand for output of existing firms.

The survey finding that entrepreneurs are part of an educated minority suggests either than education contributed to their entrepreneurial capabilities or that because of superior education they are members of the social group from which entrepreneurs are drawn. Uncertainty reflects possible differences in the economic function of education according to whether it provides economically valuable skills (the human-capital approach) or identifies talent for prospective employers (certification or information theory approach). Whatever the function, Koreans are relatively well educated, which follows both from the great esteem Confucian tradition accords education and from the enormous and highly cost-effective investment in education.

One indicator of educational achievement and the effects of literacy campaigns is that Korea's illiteracy rate dropped from 78 percent on liberation from Japan in 1945 to less than 12 percent by 1970. Elementary education was universal by the 1960s, and middle-school enrollments rose to cover more than three-fourths of the corresponding age group by 1975. Enrollment ratios in high school and college reached 41 and 9 percent, respectively, at the time.[13] By 1970, investment in education was greater, according to one estimate, than investment in physical capital.[14] Rapid expansion was possible without overburdening government budgets because public commitment was mainly limited to providing compulsory primary education, students' families rather than the government paid most of the costs, and costs were contained by concentrating on lower levels where large classes have reduced cost per student. What is unusual about the system is the early expansion despite low per capita income; by 1965, Korea's human resource development was above the average for countries with three times Korea's per capita GNP.[15]

Although the numbers are impressive, one may question Korean education's contribution to private initiative, where the stress is on individual enterprise and the capacity to originate new ideas, when schooling emphasizes rote learning and patriotism, and where "creativity" is defined as an individual's contribution to national welfare. The answer may lie in the government's attempt to distinguish social and political from economic subjects and to inculcate obedience to authority and other traditional values when dealing with the former, while promoting modern values—that include openness to innovation—in teaching economic subjects. The attempt seems to have failed, however, as indicated by continued student disturbances on college campuses since the early 1970s. More likely, the structure rather than the content of schooling provides the modern values that contribute to private initiative.

The rapid growth of the physical capital stock that has followed from Korea's high and rising investment ratios should promote private initiative as has investment in human capital. The increase in capital, according to classical economic theory, permits more roundabout methods of production that raise output and output per worker (productivity). While innovation may substitute for capital, capital stock generally expands with private enterprise, and new equipment (capital) typically embodies the latest technology and most recent innovations. The increase is visible in the national highway network (initiated during the late 1960s) and other forms of social overhead capital, Seoul's increasingly crowded urban skyline, and ubiquitous new construction. It is also a significant factor, along with increased human capital and increased technological capability, in the productivity increase as real output per worker rose 76 percent from 1970 to 1980 and more than doubled in the industrial sector.[16] Sources-of-growth estimates for 1960–1973, which allocate output growth to increasing labor, capital, and import inputs, show that the increase in capital (excluding land and buildings) accounted for 20 to 30 percent of the growth in GDP during the period.[17]

Increased investment in physical capital has generated particularly large output increases in Korea because construction costs are low and because of above-average investment in sectors where incremental capital-output ratios are below average. Low construction costs are revealed in a comparison of United States (1957) and Korea (mid-1960s) capital coefficients, which showed that U.S. capital coefficients were 24 percent higher than Korean coefficients and that much of the difference resulted from lower construction costs rather than from lower material costs or less elaborate design of industrial structures.[18] Export of Korean construction services to the Middle East during the past decade indicates that comparative advantage in construction has been maintained. The low incremental capital-output ratios, in turn, follow from limited investment in highly capital-intensive infrastructure and from relatively low outlays for housing, which does not contribute to capacity expansion.[19] Though this allocation pattern may be efficient in maximizing output per unit of capital input, on occasion it has slowed development. Electric and transport shortages during the late 1960s, for example, created bottlenecks that were strangling expansion before new capacity could be added.

Rapid acquisition and assimilation of technological capabilities have accompanied the spread of education and large-scale investment in recent years. The importance of these capabilities or the ability to use technical knowledge has been recognized, but little is known about how these capabilities are acquired and assimilated. We have no analytical framework that relates technological to economic development or identifies costs and benefits of acquiring technological capabilities, while the acquisition process seems to be largely informal so that information is scarce. However, research on technology in Korea during the past few years is beginning to reveal something about how technological capabilities are acquired and how, once acquired, they play an increasingly significant role in the economy. Though the research deals with descriptive rather than analytical issues, it has important implications for the acquisition of technological capability and for promoting innovation and private initiative in other countries.

Acquisition seems to have occurred largely through assimilation from other domestic sources in Korea, though initially technological capability must have come either from activities established during the colonial era or from abroad. A study of 112 export firms in 1976 shows that foreign sources, especially foreign buying agents, foreign-affiliated firms, and overseas travel by staff have been the major sources of product innovation but that local sources—primarily local know-how and experience acquired by employees in previous employment—have been more important in acquiring process technology.[20] These findings are consistent with an industrial sector in which competence or capability is much greater in production or processing than it is in marketing or product innovation. Though the government has increased efforts to attract direct investment in the last few years, and licensed technology imports have risen sharply since the mid-1970s, direct foreign investment (DFI) and licensing have been relatively insignificant sources of technological capability. One reason is that DFI has played a minor role in Korea's development; another is that not all DFI has contributed to acquisition. DFI is significant in the textile, apparel, and electronics industries, for instance, but has contributed little to technological development. In contrast, both DFI and licensing have been major means for transferring technology in the chemicals, basic metals, and machinery industries. However, imports of capital equipment have been much more important than either DFI or licensing as a means of transferring foreign technology.

Technological capability can be subdivided into production, investment, and innovation capabilities in which management, engineering, product or process adaptation, marketing, and other skills are combined to operate existing facilities (production), expand capacity or establish new facilities (investment), and develop less costly or more productive techniques (innovation). Capabilities are distinguished because each involves different sets of nontransferable skills and because the development of one capability has little or no carryover in the development of another. The distinctions, which are not very precise, are useful because they can be combined with trade data to reveal the sorts of technological capability that have been acquired. In particular, exports of the elements of technology (technical and management services, construction, plant exports) are evidence that investment and innovation as well as production capabilities have been acquired. Korea, perhaps the leading exporter of technological elements among semi-industrial countries, had exported $47 billion worth by the end of 1981, mainly in the form of overseas construction and plant exports.[21] The exports primarily involve "embodiment" activity (forming physical capital according to given design specifications) where comparative advantage lies not in new technological knowledge but in the organization and management of complex projects and a mastery of production engineering in metalworking and construction.

The engineering, organizational, and management skills, particularly in construction, came initially when Korean firms filled U.S. military procurement contracts in Vietnam and more recently from subcontracting in large overseas projects. Case studies reveal two basic patterns of acquiring technological capability: (1) an imitator pattern whereby local firms observe foreign technology, obtain technical information, and use these to upgrade their output; and (2) an apprentice pattern whereby Korean engineers and technicians participate in construction and operation of turnkey plants and are trained by the exporting firm's engineers. Capacity to assimilate by imitation or apprenticeship can be traced to investment in human capital and the special characteristics of Korea's educational structure. Comparison with data for four other semi-industrial countries (Argentina, Brazil, Mexico, and India) shows Korea's particularly high secondary enrollment ratio, a high percentage of engineering to postsecondary students, a high proportion of postsecondary students trained abroad, and a high ratio of scientists and engineers engaged in research and development.[22]

Though the government's educational program has favored scientific, engineering, and technical training, technological development received little policy emphasis before the past decade. New emphasis was partly inadvertent, a result of unforeseen capabilities revealed in the exports of capital goods and services (the elements of technology) that followed expansion of heavy and chemical industries during the late 1970s. (Their expansion had been intended as a means of substituting for imports.) More recently, skill-intensive (i.e., human-capital intensive) industries with export potential, such as the electronic and machinery industries, have been targeted in the Fifth Five-Year Plan (1981–1986) for expansion in the 1980s. This strategy is now being implemented by heavy emphasis on technological development; in particular, investment in a set of national research projects to develop semiconductor, bioengineering, and other technologies, liberalization of technology imports, establishment of industry research institutes, and upgrading of technology in small and medium firms. Because Korea's future export expansion is seen as dependent on the acquisition of new technological capabilities, technological development has become a matter of the highest priority.

Conclusion

Incentives and constraints that affect private initiative are examined here by evaluating the effects of government intervention and economic strategy on private initiative and by assessing the development of education, physical capital, and technological capabilities, or the cooperant factors that make private initiative an economic force. These particular topics were selected because they appear to be particularly significant in Korea, our East Asian case, but they should have worldwide significance. The role of private initiative or of individual enterprise and the capacity to originate new ideas and methods is constrained by large government sectors and highly interventionist political regimes but encouraged by economic strategies that promote growth and the expansion of the private sector. Similarly, persons with better training and greater technological know-how should be better able to exercise their initiative than those with less training and experience. Any developments that might alter government size, intervention, or economic strategy are therefore of interest, as are the factors likely to influence education, investment, and technological capabilities.

Revenue ratios and public expenditure shares, our basic indicators of the relative size of the public sector in the economy, tend to rise with per capita income but differ markedly among countries with the same per capita incomes. This indicates that a government's size is influenced by political preference and that Korea's relatively small public sector is the byproduct of a political philosophy that emphasizes output expansion rather than social goals. Subsequent regimes are likely to have different priorities, but there is no way to assess the likelihood that another regime will assume power in the foreseeable future. Though President Chun has promised elections in 1986, there has been no legitimate transfer of power since President Park suspended the constitution in 1972. The Chun regime might, of course, alter its own priorities to place greater stress on social goals. In fact, the deputy prime minister announced last January that the government is considering a "national welfare pension system," to be implemented in 1986. This seems unlikely, however, as does any significant change in Chun regime priorities. The pension system dates back to 1973 when it was enacted by the Park government but never implemented.

In a section on objectives and strategies, the Fifth Five-Year Plan notes that "by promoting competition, the government will allow the market mechanism to play its proper role" and also states that "the government will further reduce its intervention in the market mechanism through regulation and protection and will gear various new incentive systems in order to foster creative endeavours in the private sector."[23] Since the plan was released in 1981, the government has sold its equity in commercial banks, eased restrictions, and moved to lower agricultural price supports. This suggests that the government has adopted a more market-oriented strategy and is now in the early stages of what Cohen and Ranis might call a third restructuring. This restructuring has support even in government circles (which should lose power) because many officials believe that the increasing complexity of the economy makes intervention more difficult and inefficient. It is tempting to conclude that government intervention has diminished and that the economy will eventually be directed by the invisible hand rather than by bureaucrats, but this conclusion would be premature. Credit allocation is still controlled, import restrictions and agricultural price supports still exist, and the government is still interventionist by Western standards. Also, such changes have occurred before, so the pattern of strategy change may be cyclical rather than linear and what is happening now cannot be safely projected into the future.

Korea's record of rapid, export-led growth during the past two decades and the Fifth Five-Year Plan's commitment to continuing an economic strategy based on export expansion also invites extrapolation and the conclusion that GNP, the private sector, and the scope for private initiative will all continue to expand at earlier rates. This conclusion would be premature because continued expansion is threatened by worldwide recession, growing protectionism, and default among major debtor countries. As oil shocks in 1973 and 1979–1980 sparked world recessions in subsequent years, demand for both output and nonoil exports was limited by oil price increases and the deflationary policies invoked to limit inflation. In Korea, real exports rose in 1974 but fell in 1979, whereas real GNP rose from 1974 to 1975 but fell from 1979 to 1980. Where the economy grows because exports expand and exports expand because the economy grows it follows that any brake on exports will threaten growth.

Growing protectionism and debtor defaults (rescheduling) are developments that may undermine Korea's economic strategy. Export growth, particularly expansion of labor-intensive products, is limited by tariffs and increasingly by other protectionist devices such as Multi-Fibre Arrangement quotas on textile imports and the orderly marketing arrangements that have restricted U.S. footwear imports. Protectionism is becoming an acute problem for Korean exporters because the rapidity of their sales increases has triggered quota protection in foreign markets and because protectionism in the United States, Korea's major export market, has grown significantly during the past few years. Debtor defaults have raised doubts about Korea's capacity to repay loans and inspired the government, with IMF prompting, to restrict short-term borrowing this year. Though total debt has increased sharply during the past decade (to $40 billion by the end of 1983), long-term debt is modest relative to debt service capacity. Where economic strategy is linked to export expansion and foreign financing of investment in new capacity, as in Korea, any break in borrowing is likely to disrupt the strategy.

A literate and unusually well-educated labor force has been Korea's main economic asset and a major factor in its successful development. Though recession has masked underlying changes in recent years by increasing unemployment and underemployment, the combination of rapid economic growth and declining rates of population increase has altered labor market conditions. Korea, once the quintessential labor surplus economy, probably passed the turning point around 1975 so that labor is now basically scarce rather than abundant.[24] This shift in supply-demand relations and new emphasis on skill-intensive industries make education and the expansion of high-level human resources increasingly important. One may question the economic utility of an education that does not stress the modern values that contribute to private initiative. But rapid increase in the proportion of workers with secondary education, the doubling of college entrances in 1981, and high ratios of scientists and engineers to total postsecondary graduates—all indicate that the educational system is working to improve labor quality. The system has also been aided in recent years by efforts to attract Koreans trained abroad back to Korea, efforts that are beginning to offset a substantial brain-drain problem.

Investment in physical capital has been channeled in ways that maximize output growth per unit of investment. Besides the occasional bottleneck caused by inadequate infrastructure, two structural characteristics of the allocation system have constrained private initiative. One has been heavy concentration of investment in three major cities and the Seoul metropolitan area so that infrastructure in most places has been inadequate to support local industry. This is one reason why industry has been highly concentrated in major urban areas and why the search for employment has caused heavy rural-to-urban migration during the past two decades. Current planning would encourage the development of small cities as regional industrial centers, but there are as yet no positive results to go with a long history of concern for decentralization. The other characteristic has been concentration of investment in the *chaebol* (large conglomerate firms). This follows from a natural desire to lend to firms with good performance records and perhaps from a notion that only large firms can compete effectively with multinationals in export markets. The result has been monopoly and oligopoly in local markets, restriction on entry of new firms, and growing concern for restraining monopoly practices, maintaining competition, and encouraging small enterprises.[25]

The targeting of skill-intensive industries in the Fifth Five-Year Plan is beginning to alter the pattern of technology acquisition and to require new kinds of technological capability. Skill-intensive production evidently demands greater access to proprietary technology than most current production so that direct foreign investment and licensing have become increasingly important. Also, skill-intensive production depends on the sort of basic engineering and technology that have not so far been needed to export successfully. The mastery of process or production engineering, demonstrated most recently in the steel and shipbuilding industries, indicates a capacity for acquiring new capabilities. The record for obtaining proprietary technology is not so promising, however. The government, possibly because it fears domination of domestic markets by foreign firms, has done little to attract foreign equity capital whereas recent difficulties and even dissolution of Korean joint ventures make investment in Korea unattractive to foreign investors. This approach will undoubtedly have to change if the technology needed for skill-intensive industries is to be acquired.

The investment climate problem and similar problems are of interest because they provide a challenge likely to elicit observable response. Focus on problems or failures, however, should not be allowed to obscure the successful performance that has made Korea's development a possible model for other countries. Real per capita income has more than tripled during the past two decades, with relatively even income distribution. This is not the sort of statistic that conceals more than it reveals. All Koreans have benefited from such rapid development. Among the benefits, beside a substantial increase in living standards, has been the enormous expansion of opportunities for individual enterprise and economic initiative. The process seems to be reflexive, very much like Ragnar Nurkse's well-known "vicious circle." However, where the vicious circle accounted for economic stagnation, this circle has been associated with successful development.

Notes

1. From Il Sakong, *Macro-Economic Aspects of the Korean Public Enterprise Sector,* Working Paper 7906 (Seoul: Korea Development Institute, 1979), p. 11.

2. See World Bank, *World Development Report 1983* (New York: Oxford University Press, 1983), pp. 51, 156–157.

3. Dwight Perkins has argued that the Ch'ing government's share of GNP was so low (an estimated 1 to 2 percent) that industrialization failed because the government did not have the resources to support it. See Perkins, "Government as an Obstacle to Modernization: The Case of Nineteenth Century China," *Journal of Economic History* 27 (1967):478–492.

4. Benjamin I. Cohen and Gustav Ranis, "The Second Postwar Restructuring," in Gustav Ranis, ed., *Government and Economic Development* (New Haven, Conn.: Yale University Press, 1971).

5. Gunnar Myrdal, *Asian Drama: An Inquiry into the Poverty of Nations* (New York: Twentieth Century Fund, 1963), vol. 1, p. 66, and vol. 2, pp. 895–900.

6. These regimes are bureaucratic because the military rules more as an institution than through the personal rule of a military strongman and authoritarian because obedience to government dictates is required of individuals. Though the analogy is imperfect, the Park and Chun regimes are similar in significant ways to the contemporary military regime in Brazil and the former military regime in Argentina. See F. Cardoso, "Characterization of Authoritarian Regimes," in David Collier, ed., *The New Authoritarianism in Latin America* (Princeton, N.J.: Princeton University Press, 1970), pp. 33–57.

7. Leroy Jones and Il Sakong, *Government, Business, and Entrepreneurship in Economic Development: The Case of Korea* (Cambridge, Mass.: Harvard University Press, 1980), p. 139.

8. G. William Dick, "Authoritarian Versus Nonauthoritarian Approaches to Economic Development," *Journal of Political Economy* 82 (1974):819.

9. "The government developed effective planning procedures . . ." and "it was in the implementation of policy that the Park regime particularly distinguished itself from governments in most less-developed countries." Edward S.

Mason et al., *The Economic and Social Modernization of the Republic of Korea* (Cambridge, Mass.: Harvard University Press, 1980), p. 293.

10. Estimates for effective protection, export subsidy, and effective incentives (a weighted average of the first two) in 1978 are given by Chong Hyun Nam, "Trade, Industrial Policies, and the Structure of Protection in Korea," in Wontack Hong and Lawrence B. Krause, eds., *Trade and Growth of the Advanced Developing Countries in the Pacific Basin* (Seoul: Korea Development Institute, 1981), pp. 187–211. The distinction between GNP share and value-added is significant because the high import content of exports makes export ratios (i.e., gross value of exports/gross national product) an upward-biased indicator of the importance of exports in economic activity.

11. Jones and Sakong, *Government, Business, and Entrepreneurship*, chapter 7.

12. Ibid., pp. 169–176.

13. Noel F. McGinn et al., *Education and Development in Korea* (Cambridge, Mass.: Harvard University Press, 1980), p. 47.

14. The estimate, by C. Y. Jung, is cited in Youngil Lim, "Korea's Trade with Japan and the United States," in Youngil Lim, David C. Cole, and Paul W. Kuznets, *The Korean Economy: Issues of Development*, Korea Research Monograph no. 1 (Berkeley: University of California Press, 1980), pp. 44–45.

15. This finding is based on the Harbison-Myers human-resource development index, an index calculated as the sum of the second-level enrollment ratio plus five times the third-level ratio. See Frederick H. Harbison et al., *Quantitative Analyses of Modernization and Development* (Princeton, N.J.: Princeton University, Department of Economics, Research Report Series no. 115, 1970), p. 53 and Appendix VI.

16. P. W. Kuznets, "Employment Absorption in South Korea: 1970–1980," forthcoming.

17. Kwang Suk Kim and Michael Roemer, *Growth and Structural Transformation* (Cambridge, Mass.: Harvard University Press, 1979), pp. 84–93.

18. Roger D. Norton and Kee Jung Lee, "The Korean Input-Output Planning Model" (Seoul: U.S. Operations Mission, 1967), mimeographed.

19. National-accounts estimates for roughly comparable countries (those with similar climates, similar per capita incomes, and large enough populations to achieve equivalent economies of scale in infrastructure investment), such as Iran, Argentina, and Mexico, show that Korea's share of dwellings in total fixed capital formation was well below the average for similar countries during the late 1970s. It was even below that of Japan, where the inadequacies of housing are well known.

20. Larry E. Westphal, Yung W. Rhee, and Gary Pursell, "Korean Industrial Competence: Where it Came From," World Bank Staff Working Paper no. 469 (Washington: World Bank, 1981), pp. 38–45.

21. Larry E. Westphal, Linsu Kim, and Carl J. Dahlman, "Reflections on Korea's Acquisition of Technological Capability," World Bank Discussion Paper, Report no. DRD 77 (Washington: World Bank, 1984), p. 43.

22. Ibid., p. 27.

23. Government of the Republic of Korea, *The Fifth Five-Year Economic and Social Development Plan, 1982–1986* (Seoul: Government of the Republic of Korea, 1982), English version, p. 14.

24. Moo Ki Bai, "The Turning Point in the Korean Economy," *The Developing Economies* 20 (June 1982):117–140.

25. The top thirty firms produced 39 percent of mining and manufacturing output by the end of 1981 and 16 percent of GNP in 1982 and received 43 percent of total financing (*Korea Herald,* November 24, 1983, and March 17, 1984). The government announced recently that local concerns manufacturing monopolistic or oligopolistic items will be subject to price surveillance and that loan policies would henceforth favor small rather than large firms (*Korea Herald,* December 27, 1983, and January 1, 1984).

12

Market and State in Development Analysis: Beyond Normative Quarrels

Jean-Dominique Lafay
University of Paris 1 (Pantheon-Sorbonne)

The rapid growth of public expenditures and the escalation of budget deficits in developed countries have led to new consideration of the old problem of the proper, respective roles of the state and the market. The crisis of the welfare state has heavily shaken former certitudes regarding the benefits of a planned economy.[1] And this is true not only in the developed countries.

Most of the developing countries, under the influence of theoretical analyses of development economics, have grounded their own long-term economic strategy on state intervention and planning. But at least as far as the oil-importing countries are concerned, their response to what may be termed a worldwide economic crisis has been on the average weaker than that of developed countries. The prospects for catching up now appear even more remote.

On the other hand, countries with the most favorable long-term prospects are, in general, Asian countries that have turned their backs on orthodox development models relying on the planned economy. Thus, it is not surprising that interventionist policies such as government-directed investment, subsidization, and control of foreign exchange and domestic prices should be more and more contested and that many voices should now call for an extension of the role of the market and a reorientation of international aid toward the private sector.

The way economists have approached the old debate of market versus state has been slightly modified since the 1960s. First, analyses tend to be less normative, the main objective now being not only to know what should be done ideally to maximize a hypothetical collective welfare but to understand better how the two kinds of competing organizations, private and public, actually function. This trend toward a more positivistic analysis does betray more limited ambitions, but it does implicitly recognize that things often happen in the real world differently from the course envisioned in normative theories.

The school of development economics that has inspired the policies of many developing countries since the 1950s justifies a state-planned economy on the basis of two critical hypotheses: (1) The lack of rational economic behavior among the inhabitants of developing countries implies that the market must be rejected as a means of distributing resources; (2) governments can find technically optimal solutions and implement them without excessive costs.

In the intellectual climate of the 1950s, these hypotheses were so often taken for granted that people somehow forgot to ask themselves the critical empirical questions needed to support them. In fact, as we will see in the first part of the chapter, they appear to have greatly underestimated the universality of rational economic behavior and the shortcomings of the state. The fruit of these underestimations appears in the great number of perverse effects these policies have caused.

Development economics lacks a positive theory of state behavior in developing countries. I will, in the second part of this chapter, try to present the main lines of such a theory and give its consequences for the market and the public sector as they relate to accelerated development.

Development Economics, Economic Rationality and State Imperfections

Economics textbooks often justify state intervention merely by reference to terms such as "market imperfections." For example, where public goods or a monopolistic situation exists, we are told that the market will not function well and that government must intervene to correct it by regulation or even complete takeover. The achievement of some kind of collective welfare is demonstrated in theory.[2]

The drawback of this type of argument is the implicit supposition that the proposed alternative as implemented by the state will achieve ideally and without any cost what theory expects of it. This perception of the state as a benevolent despot, well-informed and acting without notable expenditures, is, as everyone knows, a short-sighted perception of the real behavior of the public sector. In fact, the state, like many markets, has its imperfections; the choice between the two types of organizations is not a choice between ideal constructs.

Economic science offers a theory of markets that purports to explain the behavior of producers and consumers, but it possesses no theory of the state to explain the logic of an administration's decisionmaking and that of the government as a whole. The justification for state intervention is limited to a demonstration that the market is in some cases inferior to a theoretically ideal state. On this unsound basis, proposals for action by the real state are put forward.

Development economics does not stop here. It stretches its reasoning to cover the whole market, suggesting that the latter is entirely irrelevant in developing countries because of special conditions that prevail in them. The poor populations of these countries will not react to price movements, the argument goes. On the one hand, such populations are thought not to have the possibility of substituting one good for another. Substitutability is limited. On the other hand, they are thought not to reason in terms of opportunity costs, so that all the various foreseeable possibilities are not compared. Their behaviors are described as mere routine, which is not rational and economic.

If the price mechanisms is unable to affect resource allocation, then only direct planning and control of the resource supplies would ensure a rapid and balanced development, according to the argument. Historically, the Keynesian influence has greatly reinforced this tendency by stressing manipulation of aggregate quantities rather than prices.

Another supposed advantage of state allocation of resources is its ability to ensure equitable distribution. Development economics attaches great importance to distribution, which it often considers more critical than allocative efficiency. This dual influence derived from Keynesian thought and from a moral preference for equal distribution at any cost is found in all areas of its analysis.

As far as international trade is concerned, for example, the following scheme results: The exports of developing countries are limited by the demand of the developed countries. That demand, largely for tropical products, is inelastic. Exports are then not sufficient to finance imports necessary for the industrial sector. The problem is made still more acute if one allows the hypothesis of an inevitable degradation of the terms of trade for primary products. Productivity gains in primary product production are then transferred by a gradual lowering of prices, while the imported capital equipment remains at a steady price. Producers from developed countries thus succeed in keeping productivity gains for themselves.

According to this hypothesis, no movement of relative prices can enable a readjustment. On the contrary, devaluation only raises the price of imported industrial equipment without affecting the exported quantities. Appeal to the state is thus deemed necessary to help developing countries use their "fixed international trade funds" and to try to increase that fund by asking for international loans.[3] The preceding model clearly justifies an autocentric strategy of reduction of imports, through protectionism and quantitative controls, as well as priority development of substitution industries.

The merits of this analysis rest on a purely empirical question: Do economic agents take into account changes of relative prices in their behavior? In a broad analysis of economic growth in the Third World from 1850 to 1950, which considered forty-one countries (eleven are sub-Saharan), Lloyd Reynolds demonstrates clearly that the role assigned to traditional behaviors needed to justify the general failure of the market in the Third World has been greatly overestimated. "There are many studies which show that small farmers, taking into account the constraints to which they are subjected, behave as economically as their American counterparts. . . . They respond to proven opportunities to increase their income."[4] Moreover, economies of developing countries, even those that have not yet "taken off," are far from resembling the stereotype of the pure subsistence economy. Their people produce and consume a large variety of goods and services. Their economies are "neither anti-commercial nor anti-monetary . . . local exchanges are always very important and long distance exchanges often very important. Individual and family businesses are not 'anti-economic." . . . Poor classes and illiterate can make their own, accurate accounts. Economy is not indifferent to innovation."[5]

The underestimation of economic agents rationality by development economics has been shown indirectly by some of the political failures it has inspired. For example, protectionist policies and substitution strategy of local products in place of imports have functioned as a subvention to industries producing imported goods, and such modification of relative prices has provoked rational reactions. Production for foreign markets has become less profitable, bringing about a significant reduction of exporting capacity. The production of consumption goods has also been stimulated to the disadvantage of the heavy industry because equipment goods were not touched by import quotas and customs duties. The free import of equipment goods has, finally, induced the choice of more capital-intensive techniques to the detriment of employment. In the same way, policies in favor of industry and the control of agricultural prices have had negative effects on agriculture because of a distortion of internal terms of trade biased against agriculture. For these reasons, many countries have been obliged to modify the policies that they adopted in the 1950s and 1960s.

Development economics has not only underestimated the extent of rational economic behavior in the Third World. It has also underestimated the defects of the tool proposed as a substitute—the state. State imperfections appear at two levels—with political leadership and with the bureaucracy. R. Musgrave proposed a well-known distinction of three principal domains of action of political economy: allocation of productive resources, distribution of revenues and wealth, and system stability.[6] Economic development policy can be considered as a policy for guiding the allocation of productive resources, in general seeking to promote a higher rate of investment than the one that would prevail naturally according to capital markets.[7] Sector by sector its objective is to attain a planned distribution of that investment.

In theory, development economics would like to adjust economic policies to attain an optimal allocation of resources. In fact, the other two objectives, distribution and stability, prevail. The main reason relates to the objectives of any government, objectives that are essentially political—the preservation of social balance, the need for justice, and preservation of the state monopoly on political power.

When there is an economic imbalance that might jeopardize the social balance, governments will tend to sacrifice objectives of allocative efficiency rather than of stability. Governments will also be very sensitive to distributive effects relative to any measure of economic policy. The distribution of "winners" and "losers" is a fundamental element in any political decision. Winners and losers might be individuals, social groups, industrial sectors, and so on.

The small importance attached to questions of efficient resource allocation may also be linked to the distribution in time of political profits that can be derived from it: A more efficient resource allocation will have long-term effects whereas certain redistributive measures might yield quick political backing. All this will in the end depend on the temporal horizon in which governments find themselves, meaning the overall stability of the political system. When stability is reasonably assured, policies geared toward efficient resource allocation, though rarely a high priority, will in general be given more weight. In contrast, when stability is not so assured, the almost exclusive objective of government will be to ensure the conditions for future stability and politically beneficial distribution, and stability will then be the privileged aspect.

As with political leadership, the behavior of bureaucracies can be a source of reduced efficiency in the allocation of resources. The economic theory of bureaucracy explains the behavior of public administration within the framework of a model where the objective of maximization of the organization's size plays an essential role (though not necessarily the sole role).[8] For reasons of power, prestige, remuneration, or indirect advantages, the bureaucracy favors larger projects than would be optimal.[9] In the domain of regulations, another field of administrative action, the theoretical scheme most often is capture theory, developed by G. Stigler, according to which "regulation is obtained by an industry and conceived and administered for its profit."[10] Stigler examines the reasons why bureaucracy tends to regulate according to the demands of small well-organized groups of producers rather than according to consumers' demands.

Even under the close supervision of politicians, bureaucrats can at least partially achieve their own objectives because they can monopolize information regarding production costs and in certain cases regarding the real demand for public goods. They can manipulate a strategy to obtain an inflated budget for the public sector.[11] Notwithstanding its technical efficiency, bureaucracy has no interest in a systematically optimal allocation of resources.

The problem is obviously amplified when bureaucracy is technically deficient. An essential element of the activity of public administration is the collection, treatment, and transmission of information. A. Breton and R. Wintrobe have shown that this imperative necessitates, beyond the individual competence of "bureaucrats," the establishment of an informal network parallel to the official hierarchy.[12] The social confidence needed to make such an informal network function is a slowly accumulated social good. For this reason, countries that lack long administrative traditions (the prime examples are the sub-Saharan countries) have trouble making their bureaucracies work efficiently. Costs for the state as a whole are yet higher.

In sum, development economics has wrongly neglected the importance of economic behaviors and the fact that the state is not a simple tool but a complex organization with its own operation costs and its own defects. As a consequence, it underestimates the efficiency of the market and overestimates the efficiency of state intervention. One may then understand why present-day economists wonder about the means of obtaining either "less state," "better state," or both. But whatever the final solution, we must not forget that there is another important factor involved here—the way the two competing modes of resource allocation, market and state, are articulated.

Articulation Between Market and State

In theory, the superiority of the market—its adaptability and its capacity for innovation—stems from the system of individual incentives on which it is founded. This system is oriented exclusively toward the increase of total production. Efficient resource allocation is all that matters; distribution and stability take a back seat.

Considering the division of labor it brings about, the market by itself is a particularly attractive solution. To avoid misinterpretation here, it must be stressed that the market referred to has nothing to do with what is sometimes described as a "gangsters' order," or that of "a 'free' fox in a 'free' poultry yard." On the contrary, the market here involves complex assemblies of rules, chosen by experience or imposed by the state, aimed at preventing exchanges between individuals that are founded on violence, as would be the case in Thomas Hobbes' "natural state." Legal guarantees of properties are the first and foremost means to put an end to transfers of goods among individuals based on force, just as the right to free entry in any market permits an end to the "natural" situation in which competitors are eliminated through menace or violence.

Market incentives lead to an increase of production because the rules regulating a market are highly general. If the state intervenes selectively, to favor or to discourage particular activities, then individuals, acting alone or in organized groups, will find it in their particular interests to spend time and resources to obtain favorable interventions. In this case, motivation to obtain government rents partially replaces motivation to produce based on the individual profit motive.[13] Technically, the terms of exchange between new production and the search for a nonprofitable distribution of the existing production are modified in a way favorable to the latter.

Mixed economies, as generally conceived, are subject to the risk of uncontrollable proliferation of such rent-seeking behaviors. Many think that by mixing the public sector and the private sector, the strengths rather than the weaknesses are summed, and the people thus benefit from the compromise. In fact, this system presents the serious drawback of building up coalitions between the bureaucracy and groups of private producers.

The problem does not lie in a risk of hidden transactions among individuals nor does it lie in the nature of the accord: The mutually beneficial solutions for bureaucracy and groups of producers will be systematically privileged. Various authors—such as J. K. Galbraith in the *The New Industrial State* and G. Stigler with his "capture theory"—have drawn attention to this problem, despite very different methodological approaches.[14]

The preceding analysis does not necessarily imply that the market should be the only means of resource allocation. It only means that the state must seek to interfere minimally in the domain of resource allocation, a domain that should be autonomous: not linked to bureaucratic objectives and the predominance of distributive or stability considerations, not linked with governments' political objectives and/

or to coalitions between state and producers. The objective is to diverge as little as possible from the goal of autonomous markets, working solely according to general rules. When the allocation obtained by an autonomous market does not conform with the wishes of the state, because of its effects on distribution or on the political equilibrium, it is in general preferable that interventions be limited to after-the-fact compensations. Only in case of very serious market deficiencies—very intense external effects or strongly decreasing costs or a monopolistic situation in strategic areas—should state interference in the market be allowed.

Even if utterly autonomous, the market is never the sole force deciding resource allocation. Public goods that the operation of the market is unable to secure always exit. Moreover, in addition to cases where the distribution of public resources is the only way, the state can even legitimately decide on the production of private goods. Though comparisons are very often unfavorable in the public productive sector, several examples prove that the state is not always an inefficient allocator of resources.[15] Here, as with the market, the difference between success and failure is often determined by the possibility of separating the objective of efficient resource allocation from other objectives.

When public enterprises are seen as principal tools of government policy, there are good chances that consideration of distribution and stability will predominate over allocative efficiency. If the public enterprise bureaucracy is the only source of information on costs in the economy, it will tend to use that monopoly to reach its own objectives.[16] In the first case, allocative efficiency becomes a secondary objective; in the second case, it is efficient from the point of view of bureaucracy but not from a collective viewpoint.

Autonomy from political considerations concerning distribution and stability is particularly difficult to achieve. An independent institution may be created, such as a central bank, to put a screen between political power and public enterprise. The creation of industrial development corporations in some countries follows this logic. Experience has shown, however, that the autonomy of these institutions is always fragile. The "screening" merely substitutes bureaucratic objectives for political ones. In other words, the essential problem of resource allocation by the public sector is not solved: Politically motivated incentives to effect distribution of wealth are replaced, partially or wholly, by the bureaucratic motivation to maximize organizational size.

Competition, when possible with the private sector, is another solution to consider. Its advantage is to render nil the information monopoly that leaders of public enterprises have on production costs. When the environment is competitive enough, the public nature of appropriation and the nontransferability of property rights do not appear to cause lower levels of efficiency.[17] An economy with two productive sectors—state and private—can, therefore, be perfectly efficient in terms of resource allocation, provided that it is not a mixed economy. The two sectors must maintain their respective autonomy.

In many cases, competition with the private sector is not possible because of the goods or services concerned. Here again, one must find the right incentives to minimize costs in order to obtain the best possible state. Some authors have proposed systems of remuneration for bureaucrats. But such mechanisms are difficult to set up. Other authors have proposed to reduce the monopoly of information of bureaucrats by inspiring an internal competition between divisions of the bureaucracy. This is contrary to traditional proposals for administrative reform that aim at specializing administrations in order to rationalize decisionmaking. But for W. Niskanen, for example, such traditional reforms do nothing but strengthen the dominant position of bureaucracy.[18] It would be better to despecialize in order to stimulate administrators to respond to appeals for the supply of public services. In other words, the idea is to replace competition "on the field" where it is not possible with competition "for the field."[19]

Finally, three conditions are needed for a better articulation between the public and private sectors:

1. The reduction of interference between both sectors in order to more closely approach the situation of an autonomous market organized by general rules.
2. An improvement of the internal functioning of the public sector that ensures a maximal autonomy of the organs responsible for problems of resource allocation and faced with redistributive and stability pressures.
3. The setting up of a system to reduce the bureaucracy's monopoly of information on production costs to prevent it from overproducing and overexpanding.

Summary and Conclusion

After a long period of domination of dirigiste ideas about economics, the market currently benefits from a return to favor as a means of resource allocation. The reason is less a better knowledge of its theoretical qualities than a real experience of the imperfections of its substitute, the state.

The development economics that inspired economic strategies since the 1950s was founded on two postulates that recent experiences have negated: (1) the absence of rational economic behavior in many Third World countries, a hypothesis that justified the rejection of market, and (2) a strong underestimation if not a total denial of the costs of public sector functioning.

Economic behaviors in developing countries are in general much more rational than has been supposed. And states are not benevolent, omniscient despots. Their chief real world defects are political priority given to objectives of distribution and stability; and bureaucratic behavior oriented mainly toward increasing the size of the bureaucracy.

In theory, the market owes its superiority to its system of decentralized incentives, which gives intrinsic priority to allocative efficiency. Since the market is a complex organization for order rather than disorder, rules regulating it should be general and decisions taken by individuals should be as free as possible from public intervention. Otherwise, the system allows the buildup of coalitions between bureaucracy and private producers, and consequently, "rent-seeking" behaviors detrimental to the whole.

Market autonomy does not imply exclusive use of the market. Beyond merely supplying collective goods, the state can efficiently produce private goods and services, when a system of incentives and adequate constraints does exist. Particularly, competition with the private sector, when possible, often suffices to ensure cost minimization. In this case, bureaucracy loses its monopoly of information on costs of production.

When such competition cannot be set up, mechanisms to counterbalance the size-increasing tendencies of bureaucracy and the low priority given to efficient resource allocation by governments are much more difficult to design. A possible solution is to set up a kind of competition within the public sector, to despecialize departments rather than to specialize them as is often done in the name of rationalization.

The need to regenerate productive activity should push an increasing number of developing countries to put the objective of efficient allocation among their top priorities. Of all the possible means perhaps the prospect of a better functioning state machinery has the best chance for rapid, concrete implementation with a simultaneous process of reduction of public interference in the private sector. Without doubt, large-scale programs aimed at reducing the state's role in the economy necessarily imply significant modifications of the status quo. Government institutions do not appreciate being detached from activities they supervise, most of all because they lose a means, expensive but practical, of acting to effect economic distribution and balance. Under these conditions, the main question is not more market and less state or vice versa but how to arrange for a better functioning state and market.

Notes

1. P. Rosanvallon, "La crise de l'Etat Providence," *Le Seuil,* Paris, first edition, 1981.

2. K. Wicksell, "A New Principle of Just Taxation," 1896, reprinted in R. Musgrave and A. Peacock, *Classics in the Theory of Public Finance* (London: St. Martin's Press, 1964).

3. D. Lal, "The Poverty of 'Development Economics,'" Hobart Paper 16, Institute of Economic Affairs, London, 1983; J. P. Berdot and J. D. Lafay, "Pour en finir l'economie du developpement," Analyses de la SEDEIS, November 1983, pp. 1–6.

4. Lloyd G. Reynolds, "The Spread of Economic Growth in the Third World: 1850–1980," *Journal of Economic Literature,* September 1983, p. 947.

5. Ibid., p. 950.

6. R. Musgrave, *The Theory of Public Finance—A Study in Public Economy* (New York: McGraw-Hill, 1959).

7. See, for example, J. Tobin, "Economic Growth as an Objective of Government Policy," *American Economic Review,* May 1964, pp. 1–20.

8. For examples, see G. Tullock, *The Politics of Bureaucracy* (Washington: Public Affairs Press, 1965); A. Downs, *Inside Bureaucracy* (Boston: Little, Brown, 1967); W. Niskanen, *Bureaucracy and Representative Government* (Chicago: Aldine, 1971).

9. See, for example, G. Terny and P. Baraduc, "Elements d'une theorie economique des organisations publiques non marchandes: bilan et perspectives," Rapport pour le Commissariat General au Plan, Universite de Paris X-Nanterre, 1980.

10. G. Stigler, "The Theory of Economic Regulation," *Bell Journal of Economics and Management Science,* Spring 1971, p. 114. Also of interest on this point are S. Peltzman, "Toward a More General Theory of Regulation," *Journal of Law and Economics,* August 1983, pp. 211–244; J. P. Berdot, "La politique de regulation americaine: les raisons de faillite," Analyses de la SEDEIS, September 1984, pp. 15–19.

11. For examples, see J. D. Lafay, "Les entreprises publiques selon la theorie economique de la politique, Mimeo IRAPE, Universite de Politiques et Management Public, 3, 2, June 1985.

12. A. Breton and R. Wintrobe, *The Logic of Bureaucratic Conduct* (Cambridge: Cambridge University Press, 1982).

13. J. Buchanan et al., eds., *On the Rent-Seeking Society* (College Station: Texas A&M University Press, 1980); M. Olson, *The Rise and Decline of Nations* (New Haven, Conn.: Yale University Press, 1982); J. P. Berdot, "Les nouveaux rentiers," Analyses de la SEDEIS, November 1982.

14. J. K. Galbraith, *The New Industrial State* (Boston: Houghton Mifflin, 1967); G. Stigler, "The Theory of Economic Regulation," *Bell Journal of Economics and Management Science,* Spring 1971.

15. See, for instance, T. Borcherding et al., "Comparing the Efficiency of Private and Public Production: The Evidence from Five Countries," University of Zurich, June 1982.

16. This point is further discussed in Lafay, "Les entreprises publiques."

17. See, for example, Lafay, "Les entreprises publiques."

18. Niskanen, *Bureaucracy and Representative Government.*

19. H. Demsetz, "Why Regulate Utilities," *Journal of Law and Economics,* April 1968, p. 55.

13

The Role of Multinational Enterprises in the Promotion of Private Initiative in the Ivory Coast

Bernard Kouassi
National University of the Ivory Coast

Just after their independence, most African countries could choose the capitalist system, the socialist system, or a combination of the two. Like the majority of the francophone countries, the Ivory Coast opted for a capitalistic system founded on private ownership of the means of production. In making this choice, the authorities conceived of private enterprise as the driving force for the development of their country. And if the results are gauged in terms of growth of per capita income, at least in the case of the Ivory Coast this strategy has been successful despite the exceptional difficulties of the last four years.

Because capitalism is based on private initiative, one might ask what role the latter plays in the Ivorian economy. What are the obstacles preventing private initiative from playing its full role as a motivator? How can private initiative contribute effectively to African economic development? Far from comprehensively answering these questions, this chapter will provide a general survey of the obstacles and opportunities for private initiative as they relate to multinational firms, employing the example of Ivory Coast.

Multinational (or transnational) enterprises are here defined as those that operate in several countries through intermediary, subsidiary companies, subjected to central control and following a global strategy. The minimum number of subsidiaries required for a corporation to be considered multinational varies from author to author. In this chapter I followed the most common definition of the minimum—two.

I have focused on multinational firms for several reasons. First, research on the role these firms play in African development is scarce. In the Ivory Coast, for example, few works on this subject have been carried out despite the fact that the Ivorian economy depends heavily on direct foreign investments (as shown by Massini et al. in 1979 and Mytelka in 1984). The subject merits attention as well because of the importance that governments and certain international organizations have accorded to relations between multinationals and the economic development in the Third World in the last ten years. Furthermore, in consideration for the narrowness of their internal markets, African countries have since independence placed great emphasis on external trade, which is generally dominated by multinational enterprises.

This chapter is divided into three sections. In the first section, we consider the obstacles impeding the release of private initiative that derive from the presence of multinational enterprises. In the second, the multinational's positive contribution to private enterprise will be presented. In the last section, we will make a few policy recommendations regarding multinationals and the stimulation of private enterprise.

Obstacles to the Promotion of Private Initiative Connected with Multinational Enterprises

The first observation that should be made concerning the behavior of multinational enterprises in Ivory Coast is that they generally follow the pattern of the international product cycle. In other words, their merchandisé is first imported into the Ivory Coast and then locally processed for local consumption. This import substitution pattern can inhibit the promotion of indigenous private initiative in the following ways:

1. The production process does not lead to the production of local inputs (denoting an absence of vertical economic integration).
2. The protection afforded to the multinational's product inhibits the indigenous production of competitive products and the creation of more economically efficient competitive enterprises.

Unfortunately, these conditions are common. The amount of indigenous production of goods and intermediary services is very small in Africa. In fact, the local production performed by the multinationals is generally very simple assemblage operations, highly dependent on imported supplies and raw materials.

Essentially, the preference for imported intermediary goods by multinationals limits the local production of inputs and in consequence the creation of local client enterprises for the multinationals. In this respect, multinationals constitute an obstacle to the release of local private initiative. Certain multinational enterprises justify this preference for imported inputs with the argument that local enterprises have problems efficiently providing intermediary goods. They blame local enterprises and especially small and medium-scale enterprises for late deliveries and the mediocre quality of their goods. Other multinational firms engaged in import substitution import their intermediate goods because they are cheaper or because they come from subsidiary firms, sometimes enabling them to profit from transfer pricing. For others, intermediate goods must be imported simply because the host country does not have the technological capacity to produce them.

Some of these arguments are well founded. However, we must note the lack of effort to adapt techniques of production in ways that utilize local intermediary goods more and the lack of effort to reduce protection that blocks out local manufacturers. In the case of Ivory Coast, these failures can to a great extent be attributed to problems with the Investment Code and to agreements signed between some multinationals and the government.

The narrowness of the Ivorian market forces the government to create conditions favorable to direct foreign investment in industry. The multinationals are accorded numerous fiscal advantages, one of the more important being the exoneration of customs duties on imported inputs. As a result of this exoneration, the multinational can produce and sell more cheaply than its local competitors (existing or potential). This competitive advantage of the multinational firms is well described by economists John Page and William Steel in a World Bank paper: "Large-scale firms [mostly foreign owned] are often subsidised through low interest rates, incentive schemes, tax rebates, allocation of scarce foreign exchange and protected from competition by tariffs and import restrictions. Such measures may give them an advantage over more economically efficient small scale enterprises."[1]

In establishing a subsidiary firm, the multinational benefits not only from the exoneration of customs duties on equipment imports (so allowing high protected profits) but also from contracts for technical assistance that accompany the sophisticated imported technology, for which the subsidiary company pays very considerable fees.

In some situations, therefore, the multinational enterprise has no interest in promoting local enterprises to supply its needs in intermediate goods. On the contrary, it would like to internalize production within the company in order to profit from a transfer pricing.

The second sort of obstacle to the promotion of private enterprise arises when the multinational's subsidiary company produces noncompetitive intermediate goods. In the Ivory Coast, high customs tariffs and the basic weakness of the market enable multinationals to fix monopolistic prices that can in turn reduce the consumption of intermediate goods or services and consequently limit the spread of competitive private enterprise in the economy.

Beyond advantages that arise from technology and preferential tariff treatment, multinational firms may also benefit from several important financial and fiscal advantages not available to local enterprises. The subsidiary company of the multinational, because it is guaranteed by the parent company, has easy access to local capital funds. It enjoys much greater trust than local small and medium-sized enterprises. Moreover, the local commercial banks are often subsidiaries of multinational financial institutions. Even the national development banks are often financed by foreigners whose loan and guarantee criteria can discourage local initiatives despite the fact that in "the opinion of numerous authorities . . . , business promoters, bankers, international experts, cabinet members, . . . the Ivorians have been gripped by a fever for enterprise creation; there are many more presenting realistic, serious projects than in the past."[2]

A survey of the officials of the business promotion organization CAPEN reveals that many realistic projects do not make it off the ground or die prematurely because the fledgling enterprise is not able to gather sufficient material on fiscal guarantee to finance its working capital. For example, a group of six young Ivorians, each holding a master's degree in business management, set up an enterprise for the marketing of food products with a registered capital of 600,000 francs CFA (African francs). The enterprise turned a profit after three months. After a careful study, these young men found that buying a truck to ensure rapid delivery would enable them to increase their market share and their profit margin. Despite their care and seriousness, the banks refused to finance the purchase of the vehicle, though a security on the vehicle should have been sufficient guarantee. According to the banks, the business was too young to qualify for such a financing.

A final obstacle to indigenous private enterprise posed by the intrusion of multinationals arises from the effects of the large companies on local consumption patterns. By securing protected markets and saturating them with their product, some multinationals have changed local production patterns and brought about a dependence on their goods. Local enterprises that produced for prior consumption patterns suffer as a result.

For example, the spread of the instant coffee of the Nestle Company (Nescafe) has changed eating habits throughout the Ivory Coast. As in many industrialized countries, the breakfast of Ivory Coast is now composed of coffee, bread, sweetened concentrated milk, and butter instead of the traditional meal of starchy foods and sauces, corn, millet or sorghum porridge.

While leading to the creation of many bakeries, this change in feeding habits has had many bad effects on the promotion of enterprises more conducive to the development of the country. This new dietary habit is based largely on imported foods, with the exception of coffee and sugar, resulting in a high food dependence on foreign countries and a loss of resources that could have been used in the promotion of local food enterprises.

Positive Effects of Multinational Enterprises in the Promotion of Private Enterprise

Multinational firms can contribute effectively to the development of African private initiative. Many have considerable unexploited potential. Multinationals' activities that favor the creation of local private enterprises or new local products and methods of production (innovations) can be grouped around three observations.

First, some multinationals participate in the promotion of local private initiative through the process of the indigenization of production. Figure 13.1 outlines the situation. The multinational firm that uses path 2 draws its inputs from local producers of goods and services. This can have a multiplying effect of creating new enterprises and new products. Indeed, the local firms that produce intermediate goods need other local enterprises to satisfy their need for raw materials or semiprocessed products. As these firms—the suppliers of the multinational firm—grow, they bring about other activities such as mobile restaurants, kiosks, and so on.

The multinational firm that follows path 3, by producing at minimum cost goods and services used by local enterprises, also contributes to the realization of indigenous private initiative. In fact, if it is not selling its product at a high monopolistic price, such a multinational enterprise can engender the creation of new enterprises because it enables those that use its goods to make considerable profit.

The second point, illustrated in Figure 13.2, is linked to the financial and technological supervision of local entrepreneurs. The Japanese example is interesting in this regard. In its industrialization, Japan benefited greatly from joint venture contracts with big multinationals such as General Electric, Westinghouse Electric, and Siemens. However,

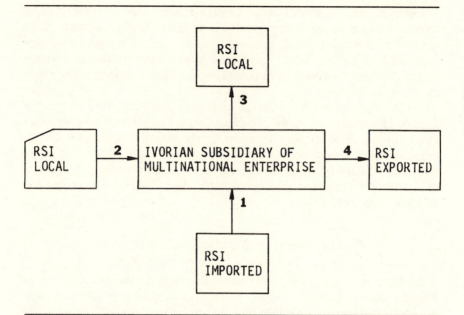

Figure 13.1 Promotion of private initiative through the process of multinational enterprise production.

Japan's excellent research and development base enabled it to adapt foreign technology to local conditions most profitably. Technological supervision by multinational firms can enable local suppliers to manufacture products of better quality and to ensure good business management. The same goes for their customer small and medium-scale enterprises that could profit by example.

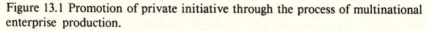

Figure 13.2 Promotion of private initiative by seeking outlets. Technological and financial supervision of a multinational firm. Note: The unbroken arrows indicate goods and services entirely or partially produced by local enterprises; dotted arrow indicates technological and financial supervision of a multinational enterprise.

Capable financial supervision would enable local small and medium-scale enterprises to reduce the cost of production of the intermediate goods used by multinationals. It would also enable small and medium-scale distributors to sell the processed products of multinationals at a lower price. Multinational's supervision of local entrepreneurs can thus stimulate private enterprise if it reduces the number of businesses that fail because of lack of modern management skills.

Beyond supervision, we must note that multinational enterprise can indirectly bring about the birth and the growth of the spirit of enterprise. This occurs on at least two levels: (1) At the professional level, the Ivorian executive employed in the transnational firm acquires management know-how, and (2) at the financial level, the Ivorian executive employed by a multinational often receives a very high salary, twice or even five times that of his or her counterpart in the civil service. This salary enables the executive to accumulate the capital necessary to finance his or her own enterprise. The skills acquired and the capital accumulated may enable this Ivorian executive to establish a business. This pattern is now common in the Ivory Coast and in many other African countries. Sales managers of large transnational firms resign to start their own businesses. In one instance, a group of Ivorian executives resigned from a multinational to create a rival enterprise.

Briefly, supervision of suppliers and clients and the training of nationals by the multinational firm can contribute effectively to the growth of private enterprise in the Ivory Coast. There are difficulties with this approach; the principal one is that the extent of skill and technology transfer by foreign experts to Ivorian executives has been limited, even though the Ivorian government has always emphasized science, skills, and technology.

A final point on the contribution of multinational firms to the release of private initiative concerns the means for export. When selling a product on the local market, any capable and well-organized enterprise can "defend" itself because the producer should know the consumer and the economic environment. However, the narrowness of African markets can and should lead many African entrepreneurs to look for external outlets for their products.

However, the establishment of export channels can be especially difficult for developing countries, above all in the area of food products. The markets for primary or semiprocessed agricultural exports are mainly in the industrialized countries, which have many regulations concerning the contents, packaging, and shipping of the commodity. It is also hard for the Ivorian entrepreneur to anticipate the tastes of consumers in the developed countries.

Faced with these problems, the Ivorian firm that conceives a new food product for export to industrialized countries has a slim chance of seeing its project realized unless it sells to large companies that know the developed countries' markets and their restrictions very well.

Recommendations

This chapter has briefly outlined the ways in which multinational companies can pose obstacles to or favor private initiative in promoting African private enterprise. By importing all their supplies, monopolizing domestic markets by means of high protection (conferred by African governments), and using highly sophisticated technology, these multinationals present obstacles to the promotion of private initiatives favorable to the development of the host country. Multinationals foster local private enterprise by integrating their production process and techniques into the economy of the host country; through their efforts in the training and supervision of entrepreneurs and the employment of competent nationals as managers and supervisory staff; by marketing local products in foreign markets. Their know-how in production, management, and marketing can have a powerful effect in the host country.

A fundamental problem that the Ivory Coast, along with other countries highly dependent on outside economic forces, must face is the evaluation of the contribution of the foreign firm to its development. Analysis of the effect of direct foreign investment must not be limited to its direct impact on the balance of payments, the level of employment, or the technology base but must focus as well on the issue of business development. Before subsidizing a multinational with long-term protection for local competition, governments must consider the contribution these firms can make to enterprise creation and the development of the domestic manufacturing sector. The contribution can be evaluated both at the level of goods and services used or produced by these firms and at the level of financial and technological supervision of the local entrepreneur and the professional training of the employees of these firms.

Notes

1. John M. Page and William F. Steel, "Small Enterprise Development: Economic Issues from African Experience," World Bank Technical Paper no. 26 (Washington, D.C.: World Bank, 1981), p. 35.

2. Koffi D. Kouadio, *La Creation d'Enterprises Privees par les Nationaux en Cote d'Ivoire depuis 1960* (CEDA: Abidjan, 1983), p. 161.

References

Bangs, Robert B. *Politiques Financiers pour les Pays en Voie de Developpement.* Paris: Tendences Actuelles, 1971.

Barnet, J. Richard, et al. *Global Reach: The Power of the Multinational Corporations.* New York: Simon and Schuster, 1974.

Brooke, M. Z., and H. L. Remmers. *Le Strategie de l'Enterprise Multinationale.* Sirey, France, 1973.

Camus, Daniel. *Les Finances des Multinationales en Afrique.* Conde-Sur-Noireau: L'Harmattan, 1983.

Johnson, Harry G. "The Multinational Corporation as Development Agent." *Columbia Journal of World Business,* May-June 1970, pp. 25–30.

Lall, S., and P. Streeten. *Foreign Investment, Transnationals and Developing Countries.* London: Macmillan, 1978.

Marcussen, H. S., and J. E. Torp. *La Cote d'Ivoire vers une Politique de Developpement.* Abidjan: Cires, no. 20–21, 1979.

14

Private Initiative and Development Strategies in Africa

Yaovi E. Randolph

Secretary General,
Club d'Afrique

"Growth, Equity, and Self-Reliance: Private Initiative in Africa—
The Challenge of the 80s" is the title of this international colloquium.
Implicitly, it asks whether we in Africa should abandon state socialism
to adopt this idea known as "liberalism"?

The antistate school developed at the University of Chicago under
the leadership of Milton Friedman is spreading around the world. Guy
Sorman's latest book, *Liberal Revolution*, is an example. Sorman shows
that the total effect of individual private initiatives is more felicitous
than the deliberate planning of government elites and that this simple
principle should "allow us to dismiss the ideological tinkerings of the
new left." Sorman points out correctly that even where (classically
minded) liberals have regained power, they have not been able to rein
in the state. It is not difficult to account for this: As we know from
Tocqueville, the people who govern the state form a real social class,
a "new class," which has become the modern expression of state
socialism and which provides its members with power and jobs. Milton
Friedman refers to this phenomenon as "the tyranny of the status
quo."

Our colloquium does not have as its primary ambition the desire
to debate liberalism versus socialism in the abstract. We simply want
to make university teachers, diplomats, politicians, businesspeople, senior civil servants, bank managers, directors of international organizations, and investors think about the present economic crisis of Africa,
to diagnose the problems and to discern adequate and equitable solutions in the context of this ideological dispute. Of course, the solution

to all these problems exceeds the scope of pure economic analysis and leads us inevitably to a discussion of politics and history. Economic statistics, however, can give an idea of the scale of the problems. Let us first situate the continent's dilemmas in the larger picture.

The population of what is commonly called the Third World is now 3.4 billion and will probably reach about 5.0 billion by the year 2000. Currently the population of the Third World is three-fourths that of the world. Yet it commands only about 20 percent of the world's resources. By 2000, the Third World population will constitute 85 percent of the world population. Today in the Third World there are at least 900 million illiterates, a figure equal to the total population of the European Economic Community countries, the United States, Japan, and the USSR—countries that produce two-thirds of the gross world product. The average life expectancy in the Third World is fifty-five years compared to seventy-five years in the developed countries. According to the Food and Agricultural Organization about 40 million persons die of hunger every year in the Third World. It is disconcerting to note that since 1960, each time the poor countries have gained $1 the rich countries have gained $268.

The situation in Africa presents an even more dire picture. In the 1950s, the mortality rate for children in sub-Saharan African countries was about 50 percent higher than the average for other developing countries—it is now twice as high. In Africa from 1960 to the present, the rate of growth of agricultural production relative to population growth has decreased everywhere. Food production has only increased by 1.5 percent a year whereas the population has increased by 2.7 percent a year, forcing the continent to increase its food imports at a rate of 10 percent per year.

Despite the rapid increase of food imports and food aid, about one out of every five Africans has an unbalanced diet, inferior to the minimum required by international health standards. The number of Africans who face serious malnutrition problems has gone from 80 million inhabitants in 1972 to 100 million in 1984.

The projections that appear in the 1984 World Development Report show that incomes per capita in the sub-Saharan countries will continue to decline from 1985 to 1995, even assuming general economic improvement. According to the most pessimistic source, the GNP would increase by 2.8 percent a year, while the rate of population growth would reach 3.5 percent; this would mean a 0.6 percent reduction of GNP per capita per year. In this case, net incomes in 1995 would be so reduced that the percentage of inhabitants who live below the poverty limit would rise from 60 percent to 80 percent in 1995.

According to the World Bank, the projected reduction of net capital flows to sub-Saharan African countries from $11 to $5 billion in the next five years is very dangerous considering the seriousness of the present crises in Africa, the degree of poverty of the continent, and the need to resolve economic problems in order to revive the process of development.

Maintenance of net capital flows at the levels reached in 1980–1982 seems to be the absolulte minimum required to support the efforts of the African countries to restructure their economic policies and revise their development and investment programs. As far as bilateral aid is concerned, the realization of this objective implies the rescheduling of existing debts combined with increased aid payments. For multinational aid, which does not allow debt rescheduling, there must be an increase in aid payments.

In Africa, the per capita product of oil-importing countries decreased by 0.9 percent in 1981, 1.7 percent in 1982, and despite an upturn in the world economy, 2 percent in 1983. Nor have the oil-exporting countries taken advantage of the economic recovery begun in 1983. Their per capita income dropped by about 11 percent in 1981 and 1982 and by 7 percent in 1983. When considering all the sub-Saharan African countries, the 1983 per capita incomes were 11 percent lower than those in 1980.

In many African countries, slight progress has been made in rural development and with import substitution industries. But without a genuine agricultural revolution offering its surplus to industries, adequate levels of domestic accumulation cannot be secured. As far as industrial production is concerned, most import substitution industries are oversized and out of line with the consumption capacity of the economic systems of African countries. They are often useless drains on resources.

Faced with all these difficulties, African countries have tended to call on the means of the "welfare state" to heal their wounds—to regulate population growth and urbanization, to ensure the expansion of education and health services, and to fight rampant unemployment. But the problems faced by African governments sometimes appear completely intractable: large budget deficits, persistent inflation, unstable balance of payments, external debts. Foreign aid cannot relieve all these problems.

Liberalism, a system founded on private initiative, private property, and freedom of undertaking and competition, can remove major economic and social obstacles to development in Africa. Indeed, for many there is no hope outside liberalism. Henry Fowler, a former high-ranking U.S. government official, once stated that private enterprise should "spread like wildfire" throughout the world. But it would seem that for Africa, with its traditions of social sensitivity and communalism, liberalism and socialism should unite and work together for the sake of economic development. This conclusion is based not only on the African experience; without state intervention, the Great Depression of 1929—the logical consequence of the continual alteration of periods of overproduction crises marking the economies of the period 1848–1929—would probably have indefinitely disrupted the world economy.

The present crisis compels Africa to revise its development strategy. After independence in the 1960s, African countries continued to produce cash crops so as to maximize their export earnings. At the same time, while setting up some substitution industries, they aimed at building large industrial units such as steel works, oil refineries, and car assembly plants. Many African countries wanted to industrialize without first overcoming the constraints imposed by the international economy. African countries, as well as other developing countries, have suffered the effects brought about by the disorder of the international monetary system and by worldwide recession. As regards financial flows, the relative drop in the value of public assistance and direct investments has only been partly offset by bank and commercial credits. Import restrictions undertaken to conserve on foreign exchange have led to a deterioriation of entire productive networks, a deterioration that has in turn hindered export capacity. The international crisis has compelled African countries to begin to abandon the idea of development through heavy industries. Africa turns to peasant populations, forgotten for a long time, by emphasizing integrated development projects starting with improved agriculture and small rural industries. Partial solutions to the present crisis may be found in the developing informal economy in Africa.

Small and medium-sized enterprises should favor the diversification of the industrial network, sectorial integration, productive use of labor, and regional redeployment. Such enterprises can ensure that an economic balance exists between towns and villages in Africa. As means of social integration, these enterprises may be able to stop the rural exodus toward overcrowded cities.

Small and medium-sized industries are especially well suited for the local processing of raw materials. Here, the Indian example is very significant. In India, the greater part of consumption goods are manufactured by such industries. Most often, they use imported methods adapted to local conditions. In Africa the development of small and medium-sized productive enterprises is feasible and promising. However, on our continent people tend to invest first in the production of the main cash crops and then in real estate. Today, the question is how to get African entrepreneurs to invest their funds in the productive, job-creating sectors. Banks and financial establishments must help these entrepreneurs set up industrial projects and find the financial means. In Africa, private banks have a fundamental role in the economic development process, especially as regards the monetarization of the national economy. The aim is to integrate the rural areas into the money and banking economies. Many African peasants still live outside the money economy in an isolation unfavorable to development.

Banks should also mobilize internal savings in order to finance development and direct savings toward productive investments. It is a question of setting up adequate mechanisms to draw household savings toward the banks in order to facilitate their availability to finance development. African banks must stop concentrating their main activities on real estate operations, where they stress the urban areas to the disadvantage of the rural areas, and favoring the big foreign companies to the detriment of African small and medium-sized enterprises.

The duty of African banks from now on is to direct their efforts toward the world of peasants and craftspeople and toward the agro-industrial sector. The banks must extend their activities to peasants and craftspeople, and their criteria for granting loans must henceforth match the spirit of African working methods, customs, and traditions. This African spirit must be felt in the banks. On the subject of risk evaluation, some authors have proffered doubts about traditional loan guarantees like mortgages, crop seizures, and peasant properties. These authors recommend instead a collective guarantee to be exercised in the framework of the village, the clan, or the family. They think that such a formula would better suit the traditions of solidarity prevailing in the African peasant's world.

Our final point with respect to African small and medium-sized enterprises is that their development and growth are inherently bound up with the development and growth of large-scale industry and manufacturing in Africa. Large units of production require a concentration of natural resources and a great diversity of equipment and technology. They also call for large investments and qualified, specialized personnel. They constitute the true "poles of growth" around which small and medium-sized enterprises are grouped, forming clusters of development. I would argue that such clusters of development must from now on constitute the prime content of any strategy for African economic development. A tightly interwoven system of large and small production units will be required to enable the 1 billion or so people who may be living on the continent in the next century to live well.

Governments have in vain tried to ensure the development of Africa. Private initiative now has to take over, to shake off the yoke of diverse bureaucracies, and to get rid of the constraints of old-fashioned regulations. Liberalism, as an ideology that recommends self-help and innovation, can help Africa emerge from its present crisis. But since the African state has always been considered the poor people's defender, the architect of the principal state infrastructure, and the founder of the major industries, liberalism and the development of African private enterprise must necessarily be allied with the African state in the effort to create the clusters of development that are Africa's long-run hope for parity in the world economic system.

Africa had its first glory days when it gave birth to humanity and bequeathed it civilization. Africans must now forget, as Marcel Proust would say, "That the only true paradises are the ones that are lost" and set itself to the task after much suffering. To seek a lost past is useless. It is equally useless to linger behind, looking for some timeless absolute. Africa cannot pretend that because of its much praised humanity, it can cease to continue its development.

APPENDIX A: Papers Presented

Author	Paper Title
Aboki, Comlan	Historical, Social, and Cultural Obstacles to the Development of Private Enterprise: Ways and Means to Overcome Them
Adamu, G. M.	The Public Sector, Entrepreneurship, and Development of Skills in the Development Process
Agblemagnon, N'Sougan	The Role of Private Initiative in Economic Development: Endogenous, Exogenous Constraints, and the Role of International Nongovernmental African Organizations
Agbobli, Edoh Kodjo	The Disintegration and the Extraversion of African Economies
Ahyi, Amakoe M. R.	Conscience Awakening, Popular Participation, and Agricultural, Revolution: Essential Conditions for Endogenous Development.
Akin-George, Chief J.	Address
Amega, Atsu-Koffi S.E.M.	An Evaluation of the Role of Transnational Companies in Developing Countries During the Second Decade of Development
Baba-Moussa, Abou Bakar	The Role of International Banks Case of the West African Development Bank
Bakabadio, Louis	A Case For Cooperatives Small and Medium-Scale Enterprise
Benissad, H.	The Private Sector and Socialism in Algeria
Bounya-Epee, N.	Actions Associated with the Transfer of Technology: The Case of African Countries.
Boutros-Ghali, Boutros	Address on Private Initiative in Egypt
Causse, Genevieve	Obstacles to the Transfer of Technology in the Field of Management: Application to Developing Countries in Black Francophone Africa

de Ulyssea, Asdrubal Pinto | Alternative Sources of Energy and Technology Transfer

du Bois de Gaudsson, Jean | On Structural and Ideological Constraint: Private Initiative and the Public Sector in Africa

Gargouil, Yves Michel | Africa and the Pharmaceutic Industry

Ghozali, Djanal-Eddine | The Operational Phase (1985–1990) of the African Industrial Development Program

Gu-Konu, B. Y. | Private Initiative and Development in Africa

Harriss, C. Lowell | Tax Strategies for Economic Progress

Hassan, Gama | The Role of National Governments in Agricultural Development in Africa

Jackson, Jeffrey L. | Bridging the Financial Gap: The Creative Use of Venture Capital in Africa

Johnson, Couaovi A. | Implications of the New Technologies of the 1970s and the 1980s for Development and Economic Growth in Africa

Kasse, Moustapha | Obstacles to Private Initiative and the Means to Remove Them

Kinzonzi, Mvutukidi N.K. | Standardization Accounting System and Private Initiative for Economic Development of Africa

Klousseh, K. | Role of the Central Bank in the Financing of Development

Kouassi, Bernard | Role of Multinational Enterprises in the Promotion of Private Initiative in Ivory Coast

Kouassi, Kwam | African Development Bank and the Opening of Capital Shares to Nonregional Countries

Kuevidjen, Kokoe Andou | Financing Women's Enterprises: Criteria for Expansion and Integration in the National Economy

Kuznets, Paul W. | State and Structural Influences on Private Initiative: An East Asian Case

Lafay, Jean-Dominique | Market and State in Development Analysis: Beyond Normative Quarrels

Lassey, S. | Constraints to the Financing of Small and Medium-Scale Firms by Commercial Banks

Luceri, Giorgio | General Considerations on Private Initiative in African Development

Magagula, Glenn T.	Rapid Population Growth: A Constraint to Improved Economic Welfare in Rural Areas of Southern Africa
Mandji, Ifefa	The Incentives of African States as a Driving Force for the Socioeconomic Development of the Continent
Masini, Jean	African Private Initiative in the Present Economic Situation
Mathonnat, Jacky	Do African States Resort More Than the Others to the External Contribution of Capital?
McNamara, Brendan	Encouragement of Private Investment in Africa
Nang-Bekale, Guy	State Incentives in Favor of Development
Olaniyan, Tsaih Folorunso	Importance of Transport and Communication in Africa in a Global Development Strategy Context
	The Problems of Training and Scarcity of Human Capital
	The Role of the Private Initiative as a Factor in Nigerian Economic Development: Constraints and Incentives in the Provision of Infrastructures
Randolph, Yaovi E.	Private Initiative and Development Strategies in Africa
Rosett, Claudia A.	Peru's Underground Market Economy (Appendix contains brief description of ILD and its authorities)
Samuels, Michael A.	Growth, Equity, and Self-Reliance: Private Enterprise in Africa—The Challenge of the 1980s
Servet, Michael J.	The Role of Tontines in Africa in the Mobilization of Popular Savings and the Financing of the Informal Sector
Skinner, Elliot P.	Persisting Psychological Dependency and Global Economic Integrative Pressures
Sossah, Fogan	Technology Transfer and Development
Thiam, Iba der	Private Initiative in Africa: A Problem of Clarity

Tshibangu, Tshishiku   The African University as a Cornerstone of
                            Technology Transfer

Tubman, Robert   The Role of Financial Organizations For Mul-
                            tilateral Cooperation

Ubogu, Roland E.   Foreign Debts and African Economies with Spe-
                            cial Reference to West Africa: Problems and
                            Possible Solutions

Velo, Dario   International Investments and Euro-African
                            Cooperation

Wagaw, Teshome G.   The Unfulfilled Role of Higher Learning Insti-
                            tutions in African Economic Development

APPENDIX B: Participants

Name	Country	Affiliation
Abotchi, Kwami	Togo	Bureau of Organization and Procedures
Adamah, Adamah Edue	Togo	University of Benin
Adamu, George	Ghana	University of Cape Coast
Addra, T.C.	Togo	Department of Planning and Development
Agbanyo, Kwami	Togo	Economist
Agbekponou, Kouevi	Togo	University of Benin
Agblemagnon, N'Sougan	Togo	Laboratoire Africain de Coordination de Recherche et d'Etudes Interdisciplinaires (LACREI)
Agbobli, Edoh Kodjo	Togo	High Commission on Tourism
Ahlonko, Bruce	Togo	Ministry of Foreign Affairs
D'Almeida, Ayigan	Togo	Ministry of Foreign Affairs
D'Almeida, Ayite-Fily	Togo	The World Bank
D'Almeida, Dosse	Togo	University of Benin
Alonso, Marcelo	U.S.A.	Florida Institute of Technology
Apenteng, G.A.	Togo	CEDEAO
Appeti, Kwami Hoboe	Togo	SODACA
Arnold, Millard	U.S.A.	Center for International Private Enterprise
Asplund, Gunnar	Togo	PNUD
Atara, Haraba	Togo	High Commission on Tourism
Austruy, Jean	France	University of Paris 2
Ayika, Leon Kangni	Togo	Societe Tropikos
de Azevedo, Maria Nazareth F.	Brazil	Embassy of Brazil
Bagnah, Ogamo	Togo	OPAT and OTP
Bakabadio, Louis	Congo	University of Marien

Bakalian, V.	Togo	Societe Generale des Moulins du Togo
Bakpessi, Matawo	Togo	SOKODE
Balde, Souleymane	France	UNESCO
Baliki, Komlan	Togo	Caisse Nationale de Securite Sociale
de Barros, Fleury	Togo	University of Benin
Nang Bekale, Guy	Gabon	Agency for the Promotion of Small and Medium-Sized Enterprises
Benoit, Jean	France	Le Monde
Bergeron, Ivan	Togo	Ministry of Planning and Industry
Berthout, Colette	France	Radio France International
Bounya-Epee, N.	Cameroon	University of Yaounde
Bourrinet, Jacques	France	University of Aix-en-Provence
Bruce, Ahlonko	Togo	Ministry of Foreign Affairs and Cooperation
Casana, E.	Ethiopia	OAU
Causse, Genevieve	France	L'Ecole Superieure de Commerce de Paris
Chona, Mark	Zambia	Sumika Investment Ltd.
Cleveland, Stanley	Togo	Societe Togolaise de Siderurgie
Dagadou, Emile	Togo	COTIMEX
Dagba, Anani	Togo	Ministry of Foreign Affairs and Cooperation
Dao, Guy	Togo	University of Benin
Dedo, Kodzo Amenyo	Togo	University of Benin
Degallaix, Serge	France	French Mission, Lomé, Togo
Delattre, Michel	France	RFI
Diarra, Salif	Mali	Chamber of Commerce and Industry of Mali
Diasso, Tanko	Togo	University of Benin
Digoh, Komlan Dzifanu	Togo	SOCITO
Djondoh, K. Assogba	Togo	University of Benin
Dufour, Patrick	Togo	Ministry of Planning and Industry
Edee, Mawulikplimi K. Agbeko	Togo	University of Benin
Edorh, Amegnizi	Togo	University of Benin

Eklu-Nathey, A. T.	Togo	SOTED
Gargouil, Yves Michel	France	Institut de Recherche Servier
Gbeassor, Ayeweanou	Togo	BCEAO
Ghozali, Djanal-Eddine	Togo	UNIDO
Golden, Myron	U.S.A.	Agency for International Development
Gosse, Hiera Robert	Togo	Banque Ouest Africaine de Developpement (BOAD)
Harrington, Anne M.	U.S.A.	Center for International Private Enterprise
Harriss, Lowell C.	U.S.A.	New York University
Hodouto, Koffi-Kuma	Togo	TOGOPHARMA
Horton, A. Romeo	U.S.A.	Opportunities Industrialization Center
Hosney, Mohamed Wafik	Egypt	Ministry of Foreign Affairs
Ibrahim, Oumarou	Niger	University of Niamey
Jackson, Jeffrey L.	U.S.A.	The Africa Fund
Johnson, Ampah	Togo	Club d'Afrique, University of Benin
Johnson, Codjo	Togo	High Commission on Tourism
Johnson, Couaovi Apan	Nigeria	OAU
Johnson, Kwawo	Togo	University of Benin
Kasse, M. Moustapha	Senegal	University of Dakar
Kekeh, K. Rohafodaye	Togo	University of Benin
Kekeh, Messanvi	Togo	Ministry of Foreign Affairs
Kenkou, Gnanri Kossi	Togo	University of Benin
Keyserlinck, Alexander	U.S.A.	International Finance Corporation
Kjellstrom, S.	Togo	La Banque Mondiale
Kodjo, Messan	Togo	SOTONAM
Kodjovi, Ayawo	Togo	High Commission on Tourism
Koffi, Kouassi	Togo	Banque Ouest Africaine de Developpement (BOAD)
Kosikuma, Blu	Togo	TOTAL
Kouassi, Bernard	Ivory Coast	National University of the Ivory Coast
Kouassi, Kwam	Togo	University of Benin
Koudoyor, Anani	Togo	AGETRAC

Koudoyor, Kangni	Togo	High Commission on Tourism
Kourouma, Ahmadou	Togo	CICA—RE
Kpetigo, Kwassivi	Togo	NCSS
Kpotsra, S. Yao	Togo	Ministry of Foreign Affairs and Cooperation
Kreuz, Leo	Germany (FDR)	Konrad Adenauer Foundation
Kuakuvi, Mawule K.	Togo	University of Benin
Kuevidjen, Nadu Kokoe	Togo	SITO
Kuznets, Paul W.	U.S.A.	Indiana University
Lafay, Jean-Dominique	France	University of Poitiers
Lare, Nadedjo	Togo	University of Benin
Lassey, Sewa	Togo	BTCI
Lawson, Chief A. O.	Nigeria	Federation of Chamber of Commerce, Industry, Agriculture, Mines and Artisans of West Africa
Lawson, Aze	Togo	Exploitation Ciments de l'Afrique de l'Ouest (CIMAO)
Lawson, Latevi-Atcho	Togo	Ministry of Foreign Affairs and Cooperation
Lawson-Betum, Latevi	Togo	Ministry of Foreign Affairs and Cooperation
Lawson-Late, Kpavuvu	Togo	COTONOU
Liaquat, Ali	Togo	BCCI
Luceri, Giorgio	Italy	Studio Consulenza Aziendale
Maier, Wolfgang	Germany (FDR)	Konrad Adenauer Foundation
Makalo, Phoday	Gambia	Member of Parliament
Suinner, Malingo	Nigeria	KAWO-KADUNA Chamber of Commerce
Masini, Jean	France	University of Paris 1
Mathonnat, Jacky	France	University of Clermont-Ferrand
Mazi, G.C.J. Okonkwo	Nigeria	Kaduna Chamber of Commerce and Industry
McNamara, Brendan	Belgium	European Community
de Medeiros, Kodjo	Togo	Ministry of Foreign Affairs
de Medeiros Lanka, Lucienne	Togo	Societe de Produits Alimentaires
Mensah, Tele Enyonam	Togo	Service Financier

Momoh, E. B.	Nigeria	Kaduna Chamber of Commerce and Industry
Moore, John	Togo	Societe Togolaise de Siderurgie
Muzorewa, Basile	Ivory Coast	Department of Planning and Research ADB
Ndaw, Alassane	Senegal	University of Dakar
Nelson, Peter	Togo	Pannell Kerr Forster
Nyasa, Citoyen Munga wa	Zaire	Association des Enterprises du Zaire, Chamber of Commerce
Olaniyan, Tsaiah F.	Nigeria	Federal Ministry of Planning
Olympio, Kwami	Togo	Department of Administration and Finance ITP
Pana, Ewihn-Liba	Togo	University of Benin
Plesch, Michael	Germany (FDR)	Konrad Adenauer Foundation
Randolph, Ablan A.	Togo	University of Benin
Kande, Samouh	Senegal	Ambassador of Senegal (Nigeria)
Samuels, Michael A.	U.S.A.	Center for International Private Enterprise
Seddoh, Nenevi Akuyo	Togo	University of Benin
Selvarajo, R.	Togo	BCCI
Servet, Michel	France	University of Lyon
Seshie, Biava S.	Togo	ATOP/PANA
Shamu, Gabriel	Zimbabwe	Delta Corporation
Sivio Koumba, Jean	Gabon	Department a la Delegation Generale Permanente du P.D.G.
Skinner, Elliot P.	U.S.A.	Columbia University
Soedjede, Douato A.	Togo	University of Benin
Sossah, Fogan	Togo	Chamber of Commerce, Industry, and Agriculture
de Souza, Ananivi	Togo	ALUREX-TOGO
de Souza, Koffi	Togo	ALUREX-AFRIQUE
Straughter, Stanley	U.S.A.	Development Assistance Consultants International Inc.

Takassi, Issa	Togo	University of Benin
Tariq, Ahmed	Togo	BCCI
Tete-Benissan, Elebu	Togo	BCEAO
Thorton, Jim	U.S.A.	Joint Agricultural Consultative Corporation
Tse, Sila	Togo	Societe Nationale d'Investissement et Fonds Annexes
Ubogu, Roland E.	Nigeria	University of Lagos
de Ulyssea, Asdrubal Pinto	Brazil	Embassy of Brazil
Van Leesten, Michael	U.S.A.	Opportunities Industrialization Center
Velo, Dario	Italy	University of Pavie
Wagaw, Teshome	U.S.A.	University of Michigan
Wai, Dunstan	U.S.A.	The World Bank
Womas, Koami	Togo	Banque Ouest Africaine de Developpement (BOAD)
Zotchi, Kodzo	Togo	University of Benin